THE
America's greatest
FLOOD
natural disaster
OF
photographed and reported
'93
by The Associated Press

A Thomas Dunne Book

Produced by Wieser & Wieser, Inc.
118 East 25th Street
New York, NY 10010

Edited by Norm Goldstein and Geoff Haynes
Text by Robert J. Dvorchak
Photo Editing by Kevin Kushel and Charles Zoeller
Designed by Tony Meisel

Printed in the United States of America by
COLOR ART INCORPORATED, Printing Division

ISBN 0-312-10795-1

First Edition
10 9 8 7 6 5 4 3 2 1

THE FLOOD OF '93

Except for the fact that the streets are quiet of kids and drays, there's really nothing good to say about a flood.

. . . Mark Twain

President Clinton and Iowa Governor Terry Branstad look out at the flood waters as they fly over Des Moines, Iowa.

On average, the Mississippi River floods every seven years on its 2,300-mile meanderings from Lake Itaska, Minnesota – where it is little more than a ditch that can be stepped across – to its mighty mouth 90 miles below New Orleans into the Gulf of Mexico.

But the 1993 deluge was anything but average. Contained to the Upper Mississippi Valley and its headwaters region, the marauding waters climbed higher and spilled into spots where no one had ever seen it before. By the time it crested at Cape Girardeau, Missouri, on August 8, an entire region reeled from the swath of death and destruction cut by the roiling waters in two months turmoil. Water-weary Cape residents bid the high-water mark a heartfelt good riddance; the town has been above flood stage every day but one since April 3.

The nine-state flooded zone resembled a mammoth inverted raindrop – 800 miles long, or the distance from New York City to Detroit, and 500 miles across at it widest point. At 55 miles per hour, it would take more than 14 hours to drive the length of the flood's path. Such widespread misery made the Great Flood of 1993 one of the worst in the nation's history. Some called it a 500-year flood – a natural disaster that has a 1-in-500 chance of occurring in any given year.

An earthquake is over in seconds. A tornado does its damage in minutes. Hurricanes build for days at sea but spend their fury within hours of landfall. A river flood had a creeping, slow-motion quality. It gathers muscle over time, lingers for weeks and releases its grip only grudgingly. While a chain of events months in the making allowed the disaster to reach critical mass, the chief culprit was rainfall so heavy that it surpassed records since they were first ledgered into the books 100 years ago. From April to the end of July, rainfall was measured in feet across the Midwest. The soggiest areas of Kansas and Missouri got 3.5 feet or more. An inch of rain on an acre of ground creates 27,143 gallons of runoff; the inundated area covered 17 million acres, or twice the size of New Jersey. The two-month period ending in July – normally a hot, dusty time – was the wettest since averages were first noted in 1985 over the states of Illinois, Iowa and Wisconsin. It was the second heaviest rainfall ever in Minnesota and seventh heaviest for hard-hit Missouri. The relentless rains conjured up biblical images of Noah and the 40 days and 40 nights of non-stop precipitation. "To get a flood of this magnitude in summer in incredible. To have it of this magnitude is unprecedented. We haven't seen anything in recorded history that's approached this flood," said Dr. Louis Uccellini, chief of operations of the National Meteorological Center, which is an arm of the U.S. Weather Service.

Half-submerged railroad cars along the shore of the Mississippi river in Prairie du Chien, Wisconsin.

A Des Moines volunteer sits exhausted on sandbags after helping to fill them near downtown Des Moines, Iowa.

More than 100 rivers jumped their banks during the flood.

Fourteen rivers reached crests never seen before – the Mississippi, the Missouri, the Minnesota, the Iowa and the Illinois among them. Other records were set on waterways that read like a geography lesson – the Des Moines, the Raccoon, the Skunk, the Squaw, the Nishnabotna, the Black, the Platte, the Grand and the Big Blue.

Those rushing waters acted like monster scouring pads on the rich farmlands of the upper Midwest. At the peak of the flooding, the gray-brown Mississippi was lugging with it the equivalent of the top foot of soil from a 5,000-acre farm each day for 17 days past the majestic Gateway Arch in St. Louis. When the river reached its highest point on August 1 in St. Louis, the largest city in the Midwest threatened by floodwaters, it rushed by at a rate of 7.8 million gallons per second. That's six times greater than the average daily flow rate. The watery avalanche made Niagara Falls look puny. The volume at St. Louis was 11 times greater than the daily flow rate over the picturesque falls.

The raging rivers humbled human attempts to harness them. Of the 1,100 levees built by farmers, hamlets and towns, 800 of them were breached or overtopped. The barricades ranged in sophistication from earth berms to creations made of concrete, steel and clay. What's more, of the 275 federal levees and floodwalls constructed by the U.S. Army Corps of Engineers, three gave way and 31 were overwhelmed. Their performance renewed the debate by environmentalists over the wisdom or folly of trying to harness one of the world's mightiest and longest rivers.

There was dramatic irony at Prairie du Rocher, Illinois, a river hamlet that fought the flood with dredges and dynamite. To save the community founded by French settlers 251 years ago, the town blasted a hole in one levee to take pressure off a parallel wall, and the gambit worked. When hearty Midwesterners were alerted the flood was coming, they

6

Why the floods?

Nearly a century ago, Mark Twain, author and paddle-wheel pilot, wrote that no matter how much mind and muscle men might pit against the Mississippi, they "cannot tame that lawless stream, cannot curb it or confine it, cannot say to it, Go here or go there and make it obey." He was right, up to a point. The Mississippi still floods and it always will, but flood-prevention projects have helped diminish the danger and damage done from floods with catastrophic potential.

Mississippi River basin

The great river network of the 2,348-mile Mississippi River gathers its water from 31 states and two Canadian provinces. All told, the drainage basin of the Mississippi system covers more than a million square miles. Heavy rainfall in one segment can send a flood crest coursing downriver.

Ohio River

Minneapolis

Missouri River
This 2,533-mile river, joins the Mississippi in a wild tide of swirling water three miles below Alton, Illinois. The smaller town of West Alton, Mo., across the Mississippi, has been evacuated due to flooding.

St. Louis

Mississippi River

New Orleans

Building a sandbag dike in St. Charles, Missouri.

Stalled weather system, heavy rains

The overall weather pattern in the United States has changed little over the past several weeks. There has been a core of hot weather across the Southeast, while the Northwest and North Central states have been unusually cool. In between, the two air masses have been colliding, setting off numerous episodes of drenching showers and thunderstorms from the central Plains through the upper Midwest and into the western Great Lakes. Since the start of June, rainfall across this area has averaged twice the normal amount, leading to the major flood on the Mississippi River.

Abnormally Cool

Flooding rains

Mississippi River

Hot

Map provided by Accu-Weather, Inc.

Sources: Time-Life Books Inc., Planet Earth Series on Floods; Accu-Weather, Inc.   **AP/Karl Gude**

nine-state flood zone, 421 were declared federal disaster areas.

The power of the flood tore at the fabric of the region. Cities like Des Moines, Iowa, St. Joseph, Missouri, and Alton, Illinois, had their water treatment plants knocked out – all were cruel victims of having too much water deprive hundreds of thousands of not enough of the right stuff for days on end. River towns that call to mind the adventures of Tom Sawyer and Huck Finn were covered with foul smelling water and muck. Even the dead felt the river's wrath. About 50 miles east of Kansas City, 962 graves washed away from 180-year old Hardin Cemetery, releasing caskets, vaults and bones into the turgid Missouri River, also known as the Big Muddy. Hours-long detours were created when the flood knocked out interstate highways, roads and bridges. Railroad systems were idled. The rivers themselves are like giant interstate highways for barges and tugboats hauling everything from soybeans, corn, grain, concrete, fertilizers, petroleum products and chemicals. The watery traffic was shut down just about everywhere north of Cairo, Illinois.

And farmers suffered. Oh, how they suffered. Over the ages, the rivers have deposited some of the world's most fertile soil ever turned by plow. But the same forces that brought it there covered it with lakes this time. Farmers along the Mississippi and its tributaries lost close to $8 billion in soybeans, corn and crops. U.S. Agriculture Secretary Mike Espy estimated that 8 million acres were inundated and another 12 million acres were too soggy to produce yields. Total farmland lost: 31,250 square miles.

Perhaps the signature moment of the entire catastrophe was captured by a TV camera in a helicopter hovering over Virgil Gummersheimer's farmhouse near Columbia, Illinois. A levee had given way on the sunny Sunday morning of August 1, releasing the river's violence in one knockout punch. The Mississippi rushed through the opening and wrenched the white, two-story house with the gingerbread trim off its foundation. Then the river swallowed it whole. "We didn't have enough sandbags and we didn't have enough men," said Gummersheimer, who was born in that house and was the third generation of his family to farm the land. Now it belongs to Old Man River.

reinforced levees or constructed new ones overnight with humble sandbags and sheets of plastic. The heroic, desperate battle was joined by the National Guard, farmers, felons on work gangs, striking coal miners, a U.S. Marine on emergency leave and a motley volunteer brigade of vacationers from France, Honolulu, Australia, Florida and Colorado. Their sweat, blisters and gnarled hands saved many places where the human spirit refused to be drowned; their tears spilled into the floodwaters in spots where their toil was in vain. The Corps of Engineers alone distributed 33 million sandbags. If each contained the recommended volume of 35 pounds each, that was more than a billion backbreaking pounds of fill in sacks lifted hand over hand, fire brigade-style.

For the record, the flood contributed to 48 deaths and caused $12 billion in damage over North and South Dakota, Minnesota, Wisconsin, Nebraska, Iowa, Illinois, Missouri and Kansas. The total tab will rise when people return to their ruined property. Although the exact amount may never be known, the damage could rival the $21 billion of Hurricane Andrew, the nation's costliest disaster. The flood left 70,000 people homeless. Of the 791 counties in the

WEATHER GONE WILD

Weather happens.

It's a pretty fundamental concept – you could ask Noah, or you could ask NOAA (National Oceanic and Atmospheric Administration) and they'd tell you pretty much the same thing: It rains, it floods, it's the weather.

You could even look up the word "weather" in Webster's New World Dictionary, Third College Edition, and the second definition would say:
"Disagreeable or harmful atmospheric conditions; storm, rain, etc."

In other words, if it wasn't for bad weather, we'd have no weather at all.

OK, fine. But isn't enough enough?

Over the past year, most Americans would probably agree, there has been enough weather, and more than enough weather, and then some.

There was Hurricane Andrew in Florida, Hurricane Iniki in Hawaii. There were record snows in the West and floods in the Southwest. There was the Great East Coast Blizzard. This summer, there's been a drought in the Southeast and no summer to speak of in the Northwest.

And of course, there have been the Midwest floods.

A few months back, people were saying that it had been a hard winter for most of the country, but the Midwest was lucky.

So much for luck.

Any one of these extreme weather events would be noteworthy – Hurricane Andrew and the Midwest floods are, after all, two of the worst natural disasters in U.S. history, THE worst in terms of financial loss.

But it's the combination that makes us wonder: Just what's going on here, anyway?

We could ask a tarot reader or a crystal ball gazer or a doomsday preacher – heck, we could ask a groundhog. But the honest-to-God, scientific fact seems to be that nobody really knows.

We asked Paul Sabol, a respected meteorologist with NOAA's Climate Analysis Center in Boulder, Colo. He stopped and thought a minute, then answered slowly, carefully and seriously.

"Gee," he said, "I don't know."

Sabol did elaborate. He said the past year had seen three "very highly significant events" – Hurricane Andrew, the East Coast blizzard and the Midwest floods, all of which were disasters of historic proportions.

But he said, "As far as a relationship between the three, I don't see any – it's just a rather dramatic sequence of events." He said he hadn't heard of any scientist who believed the three events were related.

We also asked Paul Meko, a hydrologist with the Tree Ring Laboratory at the University of Arizona in Tucson. Tree rings can tell a lot about weather patterns, because trees grow more in wet years than in dry ones, more in warm years than in cold ones.

"It seems like these types of anomalies come up every now and then," Meko said. When it comes to weather, he said, "It's hard to define what's normal ... because there's just a lot of natural variability. My guess is that this year's unusual weather is just part of that natural variability."

It is, in other words, just the weather.

Of course, knowing that severe weather is natural doesn't necessarily make it easy.

"I think it's normal – it's normal for the weather to do that," Sabol said. "It's not normal the way it affects us."

"Farmers have a saying that you can't turn your back on a dairy bull. The river is like that, very unpredictable, something you can't turn your back on," said David Lanegran, professor of geography and urban studies at Macalester College in St. Paul, Minnesota. "You can deflect it and minimize it and save parts of what you have. But the river is large enough and powerful enough to take back its flood-plain. It's like a ghost. The water is saying, `This is where I used to be. This is my place.' "

The flood's genesis goes back to the fall of 1992. Clouds pregnant with rain dumped their watery cargo on the upper Midwest. It was a relentless, cold downpour day after day after day. Soggy fields were too mushy to support tractors and heavy harvesters. Some frustrated Minnesota farmers left their corn in the fields, figuring they would have to wait until spring to get it into their cribs. That is, if nothing else went wrong.

Hundreds of miles south in Missouri, a Mississippi tributary called the Meramec River chased Richard Boyd, his wife and two children from their home near Fenton, 20 miles south of St. Louis. The fall flooding cheated the Boyds and some neighbors from spending Thanksgiving at home. A second spasm forced them to flee again at Christmas. Trish and James Boyd, ages 10 and 7 respectively, had to open their presents away from their two-story home on River's Edge Drive in a secluded neighborhood called Club City. High water this late in the year was a ominous harbinger. If the rivers were high now, what would they be like in the spring when the winter snow begins to melt and drain from the headwaters of the Mississippi through the country's midsection, Boyd thought.

When winter arrived, the Arctic cold fronts swooping down through Canada froze the wet fields and formed a frost 36 inches deep in some places. As usual, snow blanketed the frozen ground in layers 8 to 24 inches deep. In late February, the first warning signs of spring flood potential surfaced. A network of 250 volunteers in Minnesota fed routine reports of snow-pack to the National Weather Service in Minneapolis. The weather experts who keep an eye on the state's rivers dutifully marked the depths of river gauges, and they shipped the bundles of numbers to national headquarters in Maryland. The computers there crunched the data from this giant accounting system into some disturbing models. If flood potential were ranked on a scale from zero to 100, the snowpack and high rivers put the likelihood of flooding from the spring melt at 80.

The origins of the Mississippi River system are like a giant oak tree. The smallest of the creeks and streams are like the outermost twigs, that feed into scores of larger limbs that ultimately connect to the Mississippi trunk, which gets wider and wider as it churns south.

"The model tells us what we should be getting compared to what we actually had. It was telling us the system was too full," said hydrologist Gary McDevitt of the National Weather Service.

In a forecast issued February 26, McDevitt duly noted that soils in southern Minnesota were near saturation, and the Mississippi and its tributaries were above normal in the southern part of the state. The flood potential for the mainstem Mississippi and its tributaries in the soggy areas was the highest it had been in seven years. Still, the forecast called for minor to moderate flooding from the snowmelt. If it rained in the spring, the potential increased. "We knew the potential was there. But I don't think anyone would have ever guessed the amount of rain that was coming or the repetitiveness of it over a wide area," McDevitt said.

For a monster, the Great Flood of '93 had a humble birth notice. On March 3, in a six-paragraph story on page 6B of the Minneapolis Star Tribune, McDevitt's early warning was published. Because the ground was unable to hold any more water, the runoff had no place to go but into already swollen creeks and streams. "We want to alert people along the river and its tributaries early that we're watching the river closely this year," McDevitt said.

Flooding was reported March 23, at Martintown, Wisconsin, a hamlet along the Pecatonica River near the Illinois border. Flood stages were surpassed in April along the Mississippi in the Missouri town's of Hannibal – the birthplace of Mark Twain – and Cape Girardeau. In mid-April, sandbags were placed along the Rock River to protect the southern communities of Beloit and Watertown.

An army of sandbaggers in Ste. Genevieve, Missouri prepare for the worse.

The heavens opened up in early May over Marshall, a farm community of 12,023 in southwest Minnesota. In what is called the Mother's Day Flood, 9 inches of rain, combined with the fury of wind and hail, cascaded down in a single day. The Redwood River escaped its confines, creeping into basements, tearing up roads and converting farm fields into lakes. One hundred people were evacuated from a trailer court. The Redwood is a branch of the Minnesota River, itself a branch of the Mississippi. The flood in its infant stages has been set in motion. "It was like a snowball downhill from here. I did feel for the people downriver. It was inevitable they were going to have problems," said Tammy VanOverbeke, director of the Lyon County Emergency Management Agency. "When that water comes, it comes hard and fast. The power of the river puts you in awe."

But nature wasn't finished with Marshall. It flooded again on Father's Day and again on the Fourth of July. Dan and Helen Wambeke's 117-acre farm was drowned. "You look out the window and you see this black field, and you know you should be seeing something green," Mrs. Wambeke said.

The succession of blows was as hard on the wallet as it was on the heart and psyche. Such natural power makes humans feel helpless, especially when the damage is prolonged. Natural optimism only went so far for Don and Carol Louwagie, who farm 230 acres with the help of four of their seven children. "Usually, when there's sunshine, there's always smiles. Now, in order to keep them going, you gotta tell them it isn't as bad as it is. But everybody feels it. Donny feels it; he passes it on to the boys. It's very evident to me. It's really hard to pick ourselves up . . . It's just hard to go."

15

The National Meteorological Center in Camp Spring, Maryland, had been keeping a wary eye on the Midwest ever since the first warnings sounded. Then the Cray supercomputers, capable of billions of calculations per second, printed out a troublesome model for future weather patterns. A high pressure center anchored itself on the East Coast, drawing up moist, unstable air into the nation's midsection. This mountain of air, commonly called a Bermuda high, was like a roadblock; it kept systems from the Midwest from moving east. At the same time, a trough of air bunkered down over the Rocky Mountains and spawned rain storms. The rains would be locked over the soggy Midwest.

On June 5, forecasters spotted the first system three days before it hit North and South Dakota, Minnesota and Iowa. And another storm was coming just three days later. Over the next two months, a dozen storms were produced. The deluge fell in biblical torrents, water torture for an entire region.

"We realized we had a very big event on our hands, the full potential this system had. It would be stationary and recurrent, one storm after another, affecting the same area," said Louis Uccellini, chief of operations at the National Meteorological Center. Uccellini declared a critical weather day – which focuses all the computer's power on tracking the troublesome system. Such declarations are not everyday occurrences; the last one was for the March blizzard that socked the East. It alerts every forecaster in the country that something big and dangerous is coming, something that's a threat to life and property. Since the 1950s, forecasters have fed data into numerical models that form mathematical equations. The models warned of major potential for flooding.

"The worst floods in the Midwest usually occur with the snowmelt. What's incredible about this is that we are getting this type of flood in a summertime situation. There was so much rain so fast even the tributaries couldn't deal with the drainage. That

Prairie Du Rocher, Illinois, residents stand atop of a 25-foot wall of sandbags to scout the Mississippi River flood water threatening their town.

A sea of sandbags lies stacked on pallets in the parking lot of the Valle Catholic High School in Ste. Genevieve, Missouri. Many of the bags that protected this historic town have been filled here.

created pools and lake-sized bodies of water over the Midwest. It was an incredible amount of moisture, all focused on that same area," Uccellini said.

The snowmelt and June downpours left water all over the place. Wood County, Wisconsin, eclipsed ground water records set 20 years earlier. By June 18, dams built to hold back water were at their brim. The De Pere Dam on the Fox River in Wisconsin was opened for the first time in 1960. The dam released 125,000 gallons per seconds, about five times the normal flow rate. "It's a real event," said Jim Bonetti of the U.S. Army Corps of Engineers.

Other firsts followed. On the western side of the Mississippi, the first historic high water mark fell at Mankato along the Minnesota River. The water crested at 31.5 feet, 12.5 feet above flood stage and over the previous mark established 112 years ago. But most of the community was protected by concrete floodwalls constructed by the Corps of Engineers in 1969. On an east branch of the big river, the first levee failure occurred on June 20, Father's Day, in Black River Falls, Wisconsin. The culprit was the Lake Arbutus Dam, a hydroelectric barricade on the Black River 10 miles upstream near the tiny resort town of Hatfield. Spillway gates malfunctioned at the dam, which was brimmed to capacity, so water surged over the top. About 200 Hatfield residents evacuated, and emergency crews spread the word about danger over loudspeakers in Black River Falls, population 3,490. The 100 households in a low-lying area called the Grove were ordered out; some residents managed to leave only with the clothes on their backs, leaving behind reading glasses and prescription medicines. When the rush hit Black River Falls, it smashed a local levee built of clay and sand; the barrier had been raised after a 1973 flood. The water invaded the Grove, leaving only the rooftops of some homes above water. The raw force knocked out basement walls and wrenched houses from their foundations. A dozen of the homes were damaged beyond repair. Others were filled with muck and slime and destroyed everything it touched – sofas, chairs, TVs, carpeting, refrigerators, furnaces, washers, dryers, clothes, treasured heirlooms, photo albums, high school diplomas, marriage licenses, family trees, knickknacks, sewing machines and lifetimes of memories.

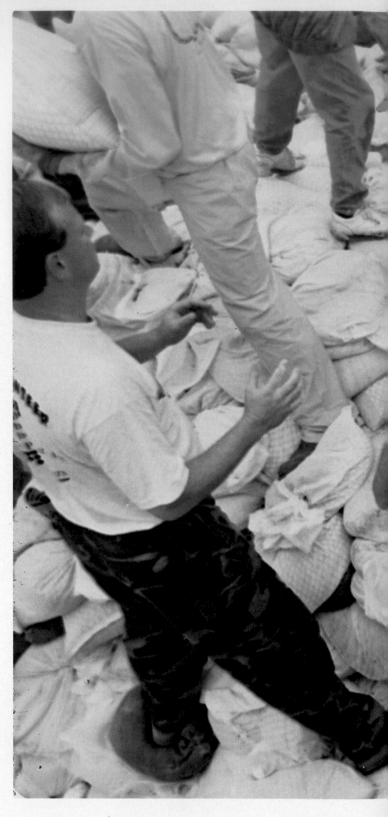

18

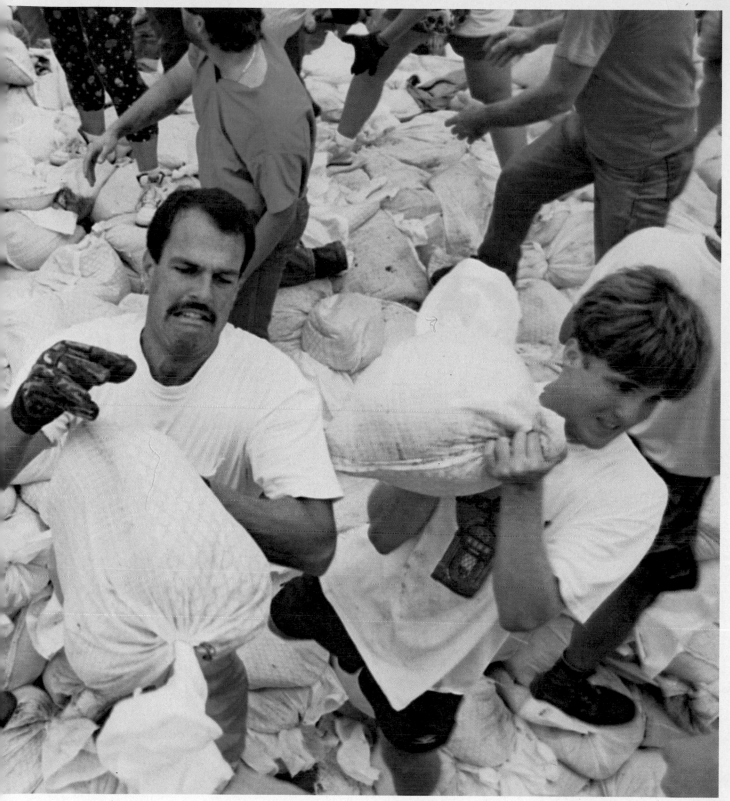

Sandbagging near the Des Moines, Iowa water treatment plant.

SANDBAGS

DES MOINES, Iowa (AP) – The lowly sandbag – standard cost, about 30 cents, ideal weight, about 35 pounds – is providing a low-tech answer to the prayers of thousands along the Midwest's surging rivers and creeks.

In Iowa, Illinois and Missouri on Thursday, volunteers worked bag by bag, shovelful by shovelful, in a sandbag brigade to keep water in check.

The Federal Emergency Management Agency said 26.5 million bags have been distributed up and down the muddy waterways of the Midwest this summer.

Sandbagging is backbreaking work. One person holds a bag, and another scoops in three, maybe four shovels of sand. The bag is tied, then hefted on a levee.

"We're pretty tired," 43-year-old Galen Mayers said as he ate lunch with his team of eight teen-agers on their third day of filling bags.

Although slow and labor intensive, sandbagging is a valuable weapon against most floods.

Sand is "very inexpensive, it's readily available in most communities... and it conforms to any shape," said Keith Haas, coordinating Des Moines flood efforts for the Army Corps of Engineers. "When properly placed and constructed, sandbag closures can be very effective in stopping floodwaters."

There is an art to this work.

"You start with a 6-foot-wide base, then stairstep up," explained David Beener of the Des Moines Water Works. Bags are laid flat, the tied end pointing downstream. Experts recommend that sandbag walls be built no higher than 5 feet, tamped into place, then wrapped with polyethylene to prevent seepage.

At the Water Works – which was knocked out by floodwaters on Sunday, leaving 250,000 people without running water – volunteers were building a sandbag ring that National Guard Capt. Ron Albrecht said would "withstand the Rock of Ages."

The material of choice for sandbags is not cloth but heavy plastic.

"Burlap has a very short shelf life," explained Kent Stenmark, natural- disaster coordinator for the Corps in Rock Island, Ill.

And what happens when the flooding's over?

"It's going to be a mess," Haas said. "What do we do with all these sandbags? Dump the sand? What do we do with all the bags?"

A member of the Curryville, Missouri, Amish community empties his boot of Mississippi River water. He and others had been walking in shoulder-deep water moving sandbags to a wall built to save downtown Clarksville, Missouri, from the flood water.

21

Elmer Simonson surveyed the wreckage of his sister's two-story home, the place where she celebrated Thanksgiving, Christmas, birthdays and family holidays. Other than the shell of the house, everything was ruined. "All the possessions, all the memories, and in a flash, it's gone. It washed a life away. Four walls and a roof are all that's left. It's like starting all over," Simonson said. In such disasters, recovery takes so long because the process takes time – drying out the walls, scrubbing the place with disinfectant, trying to get rid of the musty smell. "There were many, many tears shed down here. Each day, it's like tearing a bandage off a wound. It opens up again. It never heals. It's going to take a long, long time. But life goes on. We have to reach down to our bootstraps. We and we alone have to do the job."

When Sharon Melichar returned to her home, she found the basement walls has been pushed out. "The water came so fast it just exploded. We just stood in awe," she said. The Wisconsin Conservation Corps hauled 526 buckets of muck from her basement. The stuff was so thick that workers didn't believe the cellar had a concrete floor until they went down layer after layer. Almost all of her belongings had to be hauled to the curbside for the trash trucks – including all the mementos her mother had handed down to her before she died. "It was like I was throwing my mother away," said Mrs. Melichar, 59. "You know, I used to say all the time how much I loved my house. But I will never love it again like I did before. None of us will ever be the same as before."

Down the street, Gordie Olson's house of 23 years was gutted. In cruel irony, one of the few things he salvaged was a framed picture that read: "If The Good Lord's Willin' And The Creeks Don't Rise. . ." His son, cousins and nephew pitched in to help him rebuild from the outside in. "I worked my ass off buying this place. Had it just about paid for. Gotta have someplace to live. You can't just walk away," said Olson.

Wisconsin Governor Tommy Thompson declared a state of emergency, ordered in 200 troops of the National Guard to help with security and lay sandbags around the town's business section. As incongruous as it seemed, a boat was launched right out of city hall. Officer Phyllis Babcock of the town's police department became known as "the angel in blue" for working 16-hour days and weekends to counsel, console and comfort the afflicted.

Back on the mainstem Mississippi, the river reached its first flood crest in the twin cities of Minneapolis-St. Paul on June 26. The high water mark was 19.2 feet, 5.2 feet above flood stage, and there was scant damage. However, 400 miles of rivers in Minnesota were flooded. And that was bad news for the people downriver. The flood was just gathering power.

The Mississippi River is a natural wonder, the most important waterway in North America, the fourth largest drainage basin in the world. The basin of what the Indians called Father of Waters drains 35 states and two Canadian provinces. The drainage area covers 41 percent of the continental United States – 1.25 million square miles bounded by the Appalachian and Rocky mountains. As with anything this big, Old Man River changes personality on its meanderings to the sea. It's also been engineered with an assortment of levees, dikes, floodwalls, locks, dams and shipping channels. But the Mississippi is a maverick, and some contend it has been human folly to even attempt to tame it. The Great Flood of '93 was another painful reminder the river is in control.

The first documented flood was recorded in 1543, when Europeans were getting their first look at a continent they didn't know existed 50 years before. Explorers with Spaniard Hernando DeSoto described "a mighty flood of the great river which at that time – about the eighth or tenth of March – began to come down with an enormous increase of water, which in the beginning overflowed the whole level ground between the river and the cliffs, then little by little it rose to the top of the cliffs." It was the French who first explored the Mississippi valley and claimed it for their king (without consulting the natives who were living there). The French made the first attempt at harnessing the river in 1718, the same year New Orleans was settled. The flat crescent was prone to flooding that would erase anything built by humans, so an engineer named La Blond de la Tour was ordered to protect it. His modest first attempt was an earthen wall, 4 feet high and hardly adequate for restraining the river. A levee is a dam that runs parallel

Aquatic horseplay on a street flooded by the Mississippi River in downtown Clarksville, Missouri. Members of nearby Amish communities helped with sandbag operations; here they take a short break from the work to cool off.

Levees: the first and last defense

How levees protect lowlands and how things can go wrong, and what is done once they do

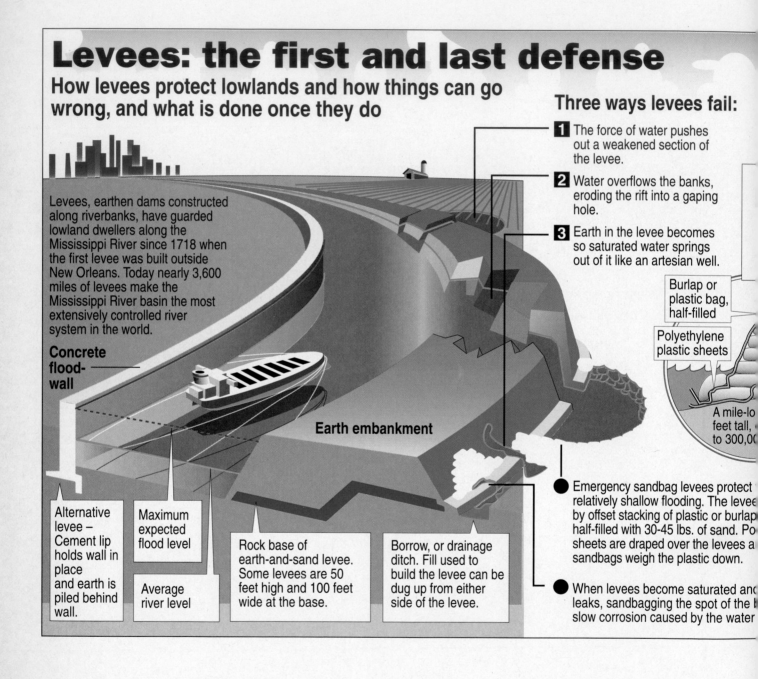

Levees, earthen dams constructed along riverbanks, have guarded lowland dwellers along the Mississippi River since 1718 when the first levee was built outside New Orleans. Today nearly 3,600 miles of levees make the Mississippi River basin the most extensively controlled river system in the world.

Concrete flood-wall

Earth embankment

Alternative levee – Cement lip holds wall in place and earth is piled behind wall.

Maximum expected flood level

Average river level

Rock base of earth-and-sand levee. Some levees are 50 feet high and 100 feet wide at the base.

Borrow, or drainage ditch. Fill used to build the levee can be dug up from either side of the levee.

Three ways levees fail:

1 The force of water pushes out a weakened section of the levee.

2 Water overflows the banks, eroding the rift into a gaping hole.

3 Earth in the levee becomes so saturated water springs out of it like an artesian well.

Burlap or plastic bag, half-filled

Polyethylene plastic sheets

A mile-lo
feet tall,
to 300,00

Emergency sandbag levees protect relatively shallow flooding. The levee by offset stacking of plastic or burlap half-filled with 30-45 lbs. of sand. Po sheets are draped over the levees a sandbags weigh the plastic down.

When levees become saturated and leaks, sandbagging the spot of the l slow corrosion caused by the water

the flooding:

...voirs along the Mississippi River system are designed to hold back
... This is supposed to counter the decreased volume ca-
... of the now-leveed river basin. However, reser-
...re kept full to promote recreational
...When the floodwater comes,
... nowhere for it to go.

...e, 5
...ke up
...

...made
...ene
...e

...g
...may

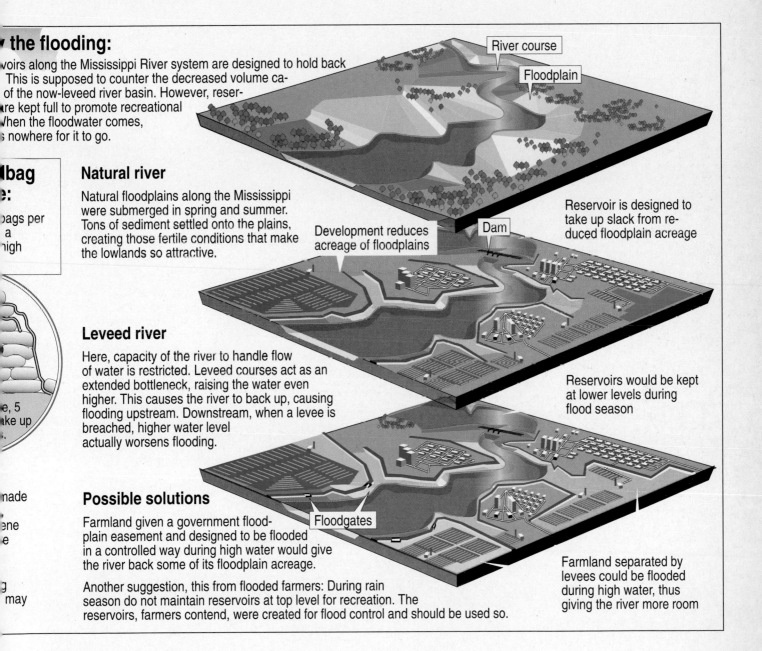

River course

Floodplain

Natural river

Natural floodplains along the Mississippi
were submerged in spring and summer.
Tons of sediment settled onto the plains,
creating those fertile conditions that make
the lowlands so attractive.

Development reduces
acreage of floodplains

Dam

Reservoir is designed to
take up slack from re-
duced floodplain acreage

Leveed river

Here, capacity of the river to handle flow
of water is restricted. Leveed courses act as an
extended bottleneck, raising the water even
higher. This causes the river to back up, causing
flooding upstream. Downstream, when a levee is
breached, higher water level
actually worsens flooding.

Reservoirs would be kept
at lower levels during
flood season

Possible solutions

Farmland given a government floodplain easement and designed to be flooded
in a controlled way during high water would give
the river back some of its floodplain acreage.

Floodgates

Another suggestion, this from flooded farmers: During rain
season do not maintain reservoirs at top level for recreation. The
reservoirs, farmers contend, were created for flood control and should be used so.

Farmland separated by
levees could be flooded
during high water, thus
giving the river more room

25

Riding the Mississippi River flood water the old fashioned way in Hannibal, Missouri. These men worked long hours sandbagging the building outside Hannibal's new flood control dike.

to the river; it keeps water from spilling over the banks, but sends it downstream to other others.

As settlers worked their way up the Mississippi, they brought their levees with them. But it was a helter-skelter system. Some places had levees, some didn't. Some worked, some failed. When disasters came, some towns would relieve pressure on their own levees by sabotaging neighboring dams. Out of this cutthroat situation, local governments organized levee districts. But only the federal government was capable of coordinating a riverwide system, and in 1849 the Corps of Engineers – whose motto "Essayons" means "Let Us Try" – commissioned the first study on harnessing the Mississippi. The Mississippi River Commission was created in 1879 to oversee river projects. Engineers decided that dams and impoundments wouldn't do much good, so they ordered more levees – which, like bureaucrats, have a way of creating more demand for themselves. In 1881, Mark Twain noted: "The military engineers of the commission have taken upon their shoulders the job of making the Mississippi over again – a job transcended in size by only the original job of creating it." Just one year later, a flood wiped out the levee system.

But it was rebuilt, and by 1922, the River Commission brashly proclaimed the levee system "is now in condition to prevent the disastrous effects of flood." A 1927 flood, which ranks among the nation's greatest natural disasters – put the lie to that boast. The angry river smashed through levees at more than 100 places in Arkansas, Mississippi and Louisiana. It was 60 miles wide in same places. New Orleans was spared only after an upriver levee was dynamited. The river flushed 818 million acres of farmland, killed 313 people and displaced 600,000 residents. Commerce Secretary Herbert Hoover raised $10 million for loans and $15 million in relief for the Red Cross, which helped get him elected president the following year. The scope of the tragedy made a lasting impression on the country. Since the "levees only" system proved woefully inadequate, Congress passed the Flood Control Act of 1928, the nation's first comprehensive flood control system that would build standardized levees and reservoirs and dams on key tributaries. In the next 65 years, the Corps of Engineers built a giant plumbing system – $8 billion worth of flood control

ODE TO THE LEVEE

ROCHEPORT, Mo. (AP) – It is a simple thing, really, just an earthen berm running parallel to a river, its wide base and sides sloping to a narrow top.

The levee is not an overly sophisticated feat of engineering or even a necessarily pretty thing to look at. But to the people of the Midwest, it can be beautiful.

In river town after river town, it was a savior, a preserver of history, the front line against the Midwest's swollen waters.

And, even on the occasions when it failed, and there were too many, it brought people together. Shoulder to shoulder they stood, day after day, night after night, hour after hour. Tossing sandbags, working together, sharing a common goal – and enemy.

"The levee and the river take on a life of their own and they assume personalities. And you become quite involved with it from an emotional standpoint. They do become entities," said Paul Davis, president of the Howard County Levee District in nearby New Franklin.

"The levee is the only thing that separates you from your temporary foe," Davis said. "And you get involved day after day and it has a tremendous impact on your emotions and how you interact with the river and the levee.

"The loneliest time is at night," he said. "You have no daylight for reference, and it's very easy for rumors to sweep through of imminent breaks. People get frightened. They take off and sometimes flee. Along comes daybreak and they find the levee didn't break. And everybody goes back to work on the sandbagging."

In Rocheport, the mood was festive as people from all over pitched in to build a makeshift barrier of sandbags; the original levee had failed during a first crest of the Missouri River a week and a half before.

The 700 people had come to the town of 250 to work, yes, but they also came to socialize, it seemed. The sandbagging took on the atmosphere of a county fair, with donated hot dogs, fried chicken and pizza served up.

"I love doing stuff like this," said Lela Moeller, who worked alongside her 8-year-old son, Kyle.

Daniel Hendron stood in his bare feet outside his home, surrounded by a towering stack of sandbags. He had emptied out the front two rooms as a precaution but, as darkness fell, the sandbags were holding.

"We ain't won yet 'til it's still back over them trees," he said, pointing to a town park that was underwater.

For him, it was simple: His personalized, make-do levee was saving his house.

"It means the world to me," he said.

Mississippi River floodwaters flow through a hole in the Sny Island, Illinois, levee flooding farmland and homes. About 2,000 people were evacuated from the 44,000 acres of flooded land.

works along the Mississippi.

But the sections of river that flooded in 1993 have fewer federal projects than any other part. Only 15 percent of the 164,000 square miles of Mississippi drainage north of St. Louis is controlled by dams, mostly because the territory is ill-suited for impoundments. Of the 250 flood control reservoirs in the entire system, 11 are located in the flood zone. "The Upper Mississippi is an uncontrolled system. It has so few reservoirs, it doesn't control anything," said Fred Bayley, director of engineering for the Mississippi River Commission.

The upper river has also been tamed to accommodate shipping. It was once a series of rapids leading to deep pools pouring into more rapids. But the Corps of Engineers constructed a system of 27 locks and dams from St. Paul south to St. Louis. The locks created a stairstep series of slackwater pools that allow barges to step up or down the river. Engineers also cleared the river of snags and sandbars while dredging out a channel with a minimum depth of 9 feet. To maintain the channel, engineers also constructed dikes, which are walls of earth and rock built perpendicular to the river banks.

But environmentalists argue these manmade contraptions make things worse. For one thing, they encourage people to build and farm on the floodplain, which is really part of the river. When the water is too full, rivers release their energy onto the plains. They're sort of a time-share apartment; in floods, they belong to the river, in dry times to the land. While a levee may protect an area of the floodplain, it deflects the water downstream to areas that need higher and stronger levees to hold back water. As far back as 1851, a civil engineer named Charles S. Ellet concluded that floods along the Mississippi were increasing in height because squeezing the river behind the levees made the water rise faster and higher. Then in 1973, C.B. Belt Jr., a geology professor at St. Louis University, published an article in Science magazine saying that the record crest of 43.3 feet in a 1973 flood was the result of flood control. "The combination of navigation works and levees causes significant rises in stages of floods. Additional channel construction and levee building will cause further problems. The 1973 flood's record was manmade," Belt concluded.

Two homes in Dutchtown, Missouri, show different ways of using sandbags to protect homes and property. The house on the left has sandbags surrounding the house and yard and is reported dry inside. The other house used sandbags to protect only the house and, according to local residents, has about eight inches of water inside. Both houses are located miles from the Mississippi River.

Mississippi River floodwaters, shown left of a broken levee, slowly flow back in the Mississippi River, right. The levee was broken by the Corps of Engineers to flood farmland north of Prairie Du Rocher, Illinois, to attempt to stop rushing floodwaters from another broken levee upstream, heading for the town of Prairie Du Rocher.

But the government disputes that. "People like Charlie Belt come out and say the Corps is making little floods into big floods. They say tear down the levees and you won't have floods. That's a bunch of baloney. If you tore them down, you'd have a reduction of two to three feet in crest levels, but you'd have a river 10 miles wide," said Gary Dyhouse, the hydrologist for the Corps of Engineers in St. Louis. The Corps argues that flood protection has saved several times the property value of what it cost to control floods.

Environmentalists also note that wetlands have been sacrificed for development. Farms and malls and housing developments now sit on spots that used to be bogs and swamps that sponged up floodwaters. The flooded states have lost 75 percent of their wetlands, according to the U.S. Fish and Wildlife Service. And in the past 200 years, 100 million acres of wetlands, or roughly half the total in the continental United States, have been squandered.

"Sadly, the states that are having the worst flooding have lost the most wetlands," said Brett Hulsey, Midwest representative for the Sierra Club.

"We've put the river in a straitjacket. That turns moderate floods into big ones, and big ones into colossal ones. It's flood damage enhancement. It's making things worse. And we're going to have worse disasters in the future," said Brent Blackwelder of Friends of the Earth.

As one of the enduring legacies of the flood, the debate may still be rising long after the waters receded.

The monstrous rains that spawned the flood turned into a killer 11 days after the heavens opened up on the Midwest. On June 19, in Benton County, Iowa, it rained an inch every 10 minutes for 30 minutes. A roaring runoff washed out a wooden culvert under Route 22 in eastern Iowa near Vinton, opening up a 12-foot deep chasm. No one can know if April Dedrick could see the washout through the torrent on the windshield of her 1985 blue Camaro. The car slammed nose first into the far wall, killing Dedrick and a passenger, Shayna Lee Stewart, who was eight months pregnant. The baby was stillborn. Dedrick, a cashier at a local food market, was engaged to Randy Rouse, a roofer. Rouse's best

An oil slick floats atop the water of a flooded street in Niota, Illinois.

friend, Chad Havens, was engaged to Stewart.

Joe Xiong's family had arrived from communist-ruled Laos four years ago to settle in Lynd, Minnesota, a community along the Redwood River about 150 miles east of Minneapolis. On June 25, the 4-year-old boy tagged along with his three brothers when they grabbed their fishing poles and buckets to try their luck in a fishing hole a block from their home. While trying to get his line further into the water, Joe apparently slipped in the mud and fell into the swift current. A brother grabbed at him but couldn't hold him. The boy was found 20 minutes later and died in a rescue helicopter on the way to a hospital in Sioux Falls, South Dakota.

Shelley Rose Epps, 11, of Kilkenny, Minnesota, drowned saving the life of her 5-year-old sister, Trisha, on June 28. They and an older sister had gone for a dip that afternoon in the Canon River, which had swelled three times its normal size. When Trisha fell in, Shelley went after her and struggled to keep her afloat. A friend, Michele Dudley, 13, pulled an unconscious Trisha to shore and began mouth-to-mouth resuscitation. Shelley, a good swimmer, somehow got sucked into the current and disappeared. Divers found her 45 minutes later, 200 feet downstream.

Among the seven people who died on the Fourth of July weekend was 5-year-old Andrew J. Sather of Wanamingo, Minnesota. He was picnicking under the secure watch of his mother on the nation's birthday when he succumbed to the violence of the Zumbro River, one of the many feeder creeks in southern Minnesota. The boy, known as A.J. and due to enter kindergarten in the fall, had gone to Riverside Park with an older brother and his mother, Melissa Sasther. His father died a year before from a heart attack. A.J. was 20 feet from the picnic table, throwing stones into the rushing water. His mother turned her head for a second, and when she turned back, A.J. was gone. The boy was found six hours

A rainbow forms over the flooding Mississippi River at sunset near downtown Hannibal, Missouri. At left are a flooded grain elevator and boat house.

36

MUDSLIDE

TACONITE HARBOR, Minn. (AP) – In just half a minute, a scenic highway along Lake Superior was transformed into a sea of mud and uprooted trees and John Larson's semi-trailer rig was ripped in two.

A rain-weakened pile of coal ash collapsed on the lake's north shore, sending tons of mud pouring down a hill onto the road.

"It was like a milkshake. It was like a wall of tree trunks and mud and water and rocks, all at the same time," said Larson, who escaped unhurt.

At least 3,000 customers were left without electricity when the mudslide swamped a substation. U.S. Highway 61 was shut down for eight hours after the 12:30 p.m. mudslide, which covered about 150 feet of the popular tourist route.

There was little warning.

"I saw it at a distance," Larson said. "The water and mud started across the road ahead of me. And then about a split-second later it was coming at me broadside."

His trailer, loaded with rolls of paper, slowed when it hit the mudslide, but kept going. The windows instantly were covered with thick mud.

"The trailer ripped in half. The tractor and the front half of the trailer kept going down with the current, and the cab tipped over. It went over real gradual."

Inside the toppled cab, Larson righted himself, rolled down the driver's side window which was above him and climbed out.

LTV Steel's nearby plant, a permanent ash disposal site that hadn't been used since 1982, was saturated by recent heavy rains and the pressure caused a dike surrounding it to break, said company spokesman Chuck Mattson.

Over the past 11 years, the dormant ash pile was seeded and inspected regularly by the Minnesota Department of Natural Resources, Mattson said. Before the mudslide, it looked like any other wooded hill.

Lists of locations from all over the country that people have come from to help in the fight to save Ste. Genevieve, Missouri hangs in the town's city hall. A 50 foot levee was constructed in Ste. Genevieve.

later. At his funeral, the Reverand Wayne Radke of the United Redeemer Lutheran Church spoke of a world in which the innocence of a family's holiday outing exists side by side with the peril of onrushing waters. "Harmless streams and small rivers become raging torrents with the ability to take life," Radke said. "But God's people do not run and hide. Hopefully, the water will go down and all kinds of frustration will go away."

Dozens of others perished in the flood. Some drowned in tranquil places like Coon Branch, Missouri, or the Otter Tail River near Fergus Falls, Minnesota, the Fox River Shores Forest Preserve, the Rock River in Illinois and the Big Sioux River in South Dakota. Some were swept away in their cars on flooded roads or drowned in all manner of accidents. Some were electrocuted touching live wires or malfunctioning appliances. Spec. Steven M. West, a National Guardsman from Ogden, Iowa, was electrocuted July 16 in Des Moines when the antenna he was putting up touched a high-power line. He was helping set up equipment for communications with water trucks. In the deadliest single incident of the ordeal, counselors Jennifer Metherd, and Darnell Redmond, and four children from a group home, Emmett Terry, 9; Tarrell Battle, 10; Melvin Bell, 10; and Terrill Vincent, 12, drowned in flash flooding June 23 at Cliff Cave County Park in St. Louis County.

Eleven inches of rain poured down June 23 on southern Minnesota. Ten inches drenched southeastern Iowa the next day. So much was draining into the swollen Mississippi that it was unsafe for river traffic. On June 25, Lock 17 at New Boston, Illinois, was the first place to shut down. By the end of the day, 215 miles of river was closed from Canton, Missouri, to Bellevue, Iowa. Shipping had been disrupted by spring floods earlier in the year, but no one could remember high water halting boats in the summer. "This late in the year, it's never happened before. Nobody plans for flooding this late in the year," said Lauren Hager, lockmaster at Bellevue. The shutdown was extended on June 26 to 500 miles of the Mississippi from St. Louis to St. Paul and 350 more miles of river on tributaries. Commercial and recreational boating came to end, partly due to

Four houses in Ste. Genevieve, Missouri, ringed by sandbags and with pumps running, continue to win the fight against rising floodwaters.

Army National Guard crewmen look out the doors of a helicopter ferrying sandbags to Des Moines, Iowa.

concerns that the wakes of the boats would further threaten soggy levees on either banks of the river. Towboat captains sought places to tie up their barges and wait out the flood. Delays cost the industry $3 million a day – the costliest shutdown in the history of the barge industry – and was the equivalent of a traffic jam of 100,000 tractor-trailers. "The boats are simply stalled in place. It's like an airline with vacant seats. Once you lose shipping days, you can't reclaim them," said Paul Warner of the American Waterways Operators in St. Louis. The Mississippi is one of the country's most important shipping routes, handling 15 percent of the nation's cargo. "The last thing these guys on a boat want to do is sit around and wait. You're just sitting there with a lot of idle time. It's like a wreck on the interstate. All you can do is sit and wait for the bottleneck to clear. There's nothing you can about it," said Norb Whitlock, senior vice president of transportation for American Commercial Barge Lines.

Among the traffic forced to dockside were the newest forms of entertainment on the rivers – riverboat casinos. The boats normally make excursion cruises. Diehard gamblers diligently trudged across gangplanks to get to pull slots, throw dice and play blackjack at The President in Davenport, Iowa, the Alton Belle in Alton, Illinois, and the Casino Queen in East St. Louis, Illinois, among other places. "The way I look at it, life goes on. People are having funerals every day. But life doesn't stop," said Loesteen Jenkins, feeding quarters in the slot machines aboard the Casino Queen. In Alton, croupiers and dealers from the Belle pitched in with their city's sandbag efforts while gamblers kept coming aboard. "This gives people an escape from what they've been fighting," said G. Dan Marshall, the casino's director of investor relations.

The second worst flood in the recorded history of Prairie du Chien, Wisconsin, topped out on June 28 at 21.9 feet, 6 feet above flood stage and way above normal for early summer. Sandbags ringed the Victorian mansion built in 1870 by fur trader Hercules Dousman, Wisconsin's first millionaire. The town of 6,000 residents, which had been the site of a battle in the War of 1812, got by with the help

41

of National Guard and a flotilla of boats that helped deliver groceries to flooded homes. "You acquire lakefront property awfully fast when the river comes up," said Veronica Duffy, whose house was an island.

Larry Kapinus wanted to work his farm outside of town, but the corn was knee-high while the water was chest-high. "There's a lot of pain out there," Kapinus said.

Two U.S. Coast Guardsmen float along the levee holding back the Mississippi River in West Quincy, Missouri.

Cleaning up after the flood

A short list of things to do once the floodwaters have subsided.

Every aspect of the house that was under water needs attention. Some examples are:

Timber: Timber (all wooden beams, lath, supports, etc.) is not necessarily destroyed by flooding. The danger comes from extended exposure to water. If the moisture level of the wood rises above 20% (up to 30% by some estimates) fungus will form. This is the beginning stage of wood rot.

Solution: Timber needs to be dried as soon as the water recedes. There are commercial firms that will provide this service and there are also powerful space-heaters that are available for rental. The key is to dry all of the wood, both exposed and within the walls. This may require exposing studs in walls that have been submerged. All mud and silt must also be cleaned from wood surfaces because it traps moisture inside the wood.

Floors: Most floors consist of three surfaces: the subfloor, which is usually made of heavy plywood or planking; the underlayment, usually made of thin plywood, masonite or particle board; and the surface, usually either vinyl or carpeting. Hardwood floors generally are made in two layers, the subfloor and the hardwood surface. The surface layer and underlayment will need replacement if soaked with water. Carpeting and vinyl backings fall apart when soaked and cannot be salvaged. Particle board is ruined by exposure to water. Thin plywood will most often warp and become unusable.

Walls:

Plaster walls: Plaster walls essentially are a form of cement. Water usually will not destroy it. However, the wooden frames within the walls must be dried. This usually requires most, if not all of the plaster, to be removed in order to dry the timber and lath. Plaster walls that have sustained only surface damage can be scrubbed down and repainted.

Sheetrock (wallboard): When submerged for any period of time, this material may crumble away. If the wall does not fall apart, it may absorb a great deal of moisture. When it dries out, it probably will warp and deform. The best suggestion is to remove the remaining wall board and dry the timbers. If the wall is not too badly damaged, it can be cleaned and repainted.

Plumbing: Most systems will weather the flood with little or no damage. They are meant for water conditions. Some low-lying pipes may need flushing out to remove any mud or silt that may have collected.

Electrical: Water should not damage insulated wiring. Critical attention to restoring an electrical system lies in cleaning out and drying all junction boxes, receptacles, fixtures and, most importantly, the fuse or circuit box. Each of these aspects of the system must be disassembled, cleaned and dried long before any electricity can be restored. Exposed wire will corrode if not properly dried. Connections must be examined. All electrical fixtures (lamps, appliances, etc.) must be taken apart and cleaned in the same way.

Heating:

Gas heat: Gas is a closed system and remains essentially water-tight. All gas appliances have motors that must be completely taken apart, cleaned and dried or replaced. Stoves, clothes dryers, gas heaters and water heaters that have been submerged need to be disassembled and cleaned. Burners (and pilots) need particular attention. The small holes tend to fill with mud and debris and will not function properly unless completely cleaned.

Oil heat: Most oil tanks will remain watertight. If water seeps into an oil tank the local supplier can remove it. In both oil and gas systems, the motors of each appliance are the most vulnerable.

Source: The Carey Bros.

AP/William J. Castello, John Monahan, Brian Sipple

A Portage Des Sioux, Missouri, resident holds a suitcase overhead as he wades through flood water to a National Guard truck. The National Guard provided a shuttle service for residents needing to return to, or leave, the isolated town.

Davenport, Iowa, is the largest city on the Mississippi River without a floodwall. Three times since the city of 95,000 hit record floods in 1965, the city council voted against building a levee because it would ruin the view of the river. Its neighbors in an area called Quad Cities – Bettendorf, Iowa, and Rock Island, Illinois – opted for floodwalls and remained relatively unscathed.

But the flood bore down on downtown Davenport in late June and early July. The city filled and stacked 300,000 sandbags with the help of businessmen, volunteers and the Iowa National Guard. The unspoiled, spectacular view of the river was closer than anyone had ever seen it. Water surged three or four blocks deep and 10 blocks wide into the downtown business section. The scenic River Drive lived up to its name – it was submerged underwater, accessible only by boat.

'It's an absolute disgrace Davenport does not have a flood wall. A few purists don't want to ruin the view of the river. This is 1993, not 1793," said Steve Hagge, whose furniture store was shut down and had fish swimming in the basement. Ultimately, the river topped out at an all-time high of 22.5 feet – 7 feet over flood stage.

One of the most visible casualties of the flood was Davenport's minor league baseball team, which has been part of the city's history since 1889. But the Quad City River Bandits' municipal stadium was buried under water and accessible only by boat. The team, which stands to lose $500,000 in the flood, found an alternative playing field 10 miles away in Eldredge – a high school diamond with a soybean field along the left field line in the heart of Iowa farm country. The team printed up T-shirts reading 'Field of Streams" and joked of holding a jet ski tournament in their old parking lot. (The real 'Field of Dreams" carved out of an Iowa cornfield by Hollywood movie-makers remained untouched by the floods in Dyersville.)

Greg Kehl became a river refugee with a lot less fanfare. When a soggy levee threatened to give way in his Davenport neighborhood, Kehl fled to a Red Cross shelter and then began living in a van so he could keep his pets – Molly the dog and Blackie the cat – with him. 'There's a dark cloud over Iowa. It

RADIO LINKS

STE. GENEVIEVE, Mo. (AP) – There's a comforting sound blending with the thump of sandbags and the roar of water pumps in the flooded Midwest. It's the personal, portable companionship of constant radio coverage.

"This is radio at its finest," said Bob Scott, general manager of KSGM-AM in Ste. Genevieve, which broadcast continuous flood coverage for three weeks until a levee break inundated the station's transmitter.

"I stood there and watched the water surround our towers and cover the transmitter building. It was a sad, sad sight. But we switched to our FM station and kept fighting," Scott said.

Neighbors and visitors paused at 1:30 each afternoon as sister station KBDZ-FM carries emergency authorities' daily flood briefing live from City Hall. The stations also put a portable transmitter there, and officials may seize the airwaves anytime to relay new information.

"I just keep close to the radio," said Rosalie Schweigert, 67, who has resisted three evacuation orders and lives near a levee here. She can stand on her front porch and see floodwaters slosh about 20 yards away.

Mrs. Schweigert and her disabled husband have their car packed "and can leave in 10 minutes if they tell us on the radio to do so."

"You might say it's been our lifeline," she said.

Across the Midwest, radio stations with formats from rock to religious have dumped programming and advertising to provide fast updates on flooding — often from the scene.

WGEM radio and television started continuous broadcasts from Quincy, Ill., on July 1 with the slogan, "Flood Command Center."

"With radio, you pick up a cellular phone and broadcast from the levee," said Leo Henning, the stations' director of operations.

The WGEM crew began to relax after the Mississippi River's crest passed Quincy last week, but that changed Sunday when the Sny Island Levee was breached.

"It's the story of the century," said morning news anchor Bob Turek.

Downriver at St. Louis, powerhouse news-talk station KMOX-AM ran "Floodcenter" reports each hour, "with bulletins at once," said program director Tom Langmyer. The station's 50,000-watt signal reaches across the Midwest in the daytime and to 46 states at night.

KMOX added a second helicopter to cover the floods, summoned reporters from other CBS-owned stations in New York and Chicago and wheeled in a radio satellite truck. The station set up a listener line to connect flood victims with services and sponsored a St. Louis Symphony benefit that raised $65,000 for the American Red Cross.

Aware of their large and loyal audiences, President Clinton did live interviews from Air Force One with WGEM and KMOX during his trips to inspect flood damage. The president also took listener questions at WHO-AM in Des Moines on a program carried by KMOX and WCCO-AM in Minneapolis.

Such sweeping coverage costs money. Langmyer, for example, said the KMOX tab will push into tens of thousands of dollars at least.

But broadcasters said they reap a long-term benefit in listener loyalty. And, after all, this is just what you do.

"This really is the whole point of the radio business," said Dave Bartlett, president of the Washington-based Radio-Television News Directors Association.

"If you don't help the listener in bad times," he said, "how can you expect them to turn to you in the good times?"

A nurse's aid at the Community Care Center of Lemay, Missouri, wraps a resident of the center in a blanket during an evacuation of the center. The evacuation was a precaution against unstable propane tanks floating in the floodwaters near St. Louis. Some 8,000 others were also evacuated.

matches everybody's feelings, frustrations and stress," said Kehl, a self-employed handyman who said he's never going back to his old home. 'Ever since this thing started, we've been living through hell. And we're going to be there a little while longer. We have no other place to go." At one point, as sodden skies continued to splash down day after day after day, Kehl looked heavenward and screamed: 'Make it stop. Enough's enough."

The cruel paradox of having too much water but not enough of the right stuff knocked Des Moines flat. The Raccoon River overwhelmed a 15-foot high dike and swamped the city's treatment plant early on Sunday, July 11, leaving 250,000 people with no water for drinking, showering or flushing for 12 grueling days. Queues formed at water distribution sites and makeshift public showers while donations of bottled water poured in from all over the country. President Clinton returned from the Tokyo summit and a vacation in Hawaii to tour the area.

At one of the water points in a supermarket parking lot, Clinton encountered Christina Hein, a computer operator. She broke down in tears and cried: 'We just can't take anymore." The most powerful man in the world, unable to control the flood, squeezed her right hand and put his arm around her shoulders. 'Hang in there," he comforted her.

With the city's 810 miles of mains and pipes filled with contaminated water, life limped on. Doctors at Mercy Hospital Medical Center delivered 10 babies – one by Caesarean section without running water, one by flashlight. 'You can't stop babies. They just keep coming, no matter what," said Mary Biggs, a nurse. The unflagging Midwestern spirit surfaced above the deluge. Fran Van Winkle, a 72-year-old patient in the cancer unit, described it this way: 'Whatever it is that hits, it can be solved. It's a foregone conclusion that it can be solved."

Residents changed their state motto from "Iowa – A Place To Grow" to "Iowa – A Place to Row." The city's zip code was jokingly listed as 50H2O. The Des Moines *Register*, forced to moved its newsroom to a suburban motel, ran an 'I'm a Floody Mess" contest, trying to keep the city's spirits up after the water system failed. Subscribers completed joke sentences ('I smell so bad ..." 'My clothes are so dirty ...").

A Grafton, Illinois, fireman carries a woman to a stretcher. She suffers from Lou Gehrig's Disease and was stranded by the flooding Illinois river.

Portage Des Sioux, Missouri, resident and her dog ride a National Guard truck out of the flooded town.

A woman and her cat have a tearful reunion in St. Louis, Missouri. Left behind when her owner was forced to evacuate their home, the cat was rescued by Humane Society workers.

Among the hundreds of replies was Pat Jarvinen's: 'I smell so bad that my Sure deodorant is undecided." Tom Rowles' entry was: 'It was so wet that ... dry humor was appreciated."

Midwest gumption was symbolized by the 1,100 residents of Eddyville, Iowa, who moved their bank, post office and city clerk's office to the high school and were determined to get on with their lives despite Des Moines River flooding that caused an estimated $2 million in damage, more than five times the city's annual budget. 'These people just aren't going to give up," said Mayor Ken Carr. 'They would try to sandbag this place even if it were under water."

But when the Mississippi reached its reached in Keokuk, the southernmost town in Iowa, Governor Terry Branstad said: 'It's the worst natural disaster we've ever had."

The flood had already ravaged parts of Missouri and Illinois before throwing its mightiest punch. Vice President Al Gore visited Grafton, Illinois, where a sign in Grandma's Kitchen Restaurant read: 'Noah would have eaten here." Gore had flown over the stricken region, shocked at the sight of a mammoth, gray-green lake formed by the malicious Mississippi. 'Unbelievable," Gore said. 'You can't even tell where the Mississippi begins and the farmland ends." Fran Woertz of St. Peters, Missouri, noted: 'This isn't a river, it's an ocean."

Given advance warning of flooding, people downriver began a heroic and furious struggle to shore up floodwalls. The signature piece of equipment was the humble sandbag, made of burlap or woven polypropylene – a sack of plastic costing about 22 cents. A surplus of the sandbags was left over from Desert Storm, where they were designed to stop bullets and shrapnel in the mother of all battles. Now they made overnight fortresses in the fight against the Father of Waters. It took 25,000 sandbags, weighing 35 pounds apiece, to add one foot to a one mile section of levee. A backbreaking ritual was played out under the sodden skies. Bend, scoop, lift, fill, tie, grab, fling, pass, pass, pass, place. In many places, an American flag was planted on levees to buoy volunteer spirits. KMOX, the superstation in St. Louis, broadcast the need for sandbaggers and volunteers seemed to materialize instantly at staging areas. Hog

farmers toiled shoulder-to-shoulder with city slickers. Amishmen in their straw hats, long-sleeved cotton shirts and suspendered black trousers contrasted with college students wearing shorts and sneaker and National Guard in camouflage fatigues and combat boots. Prison work gangs joined the struggle at places like Niota, Illinois. At West Quincy, Missouri, 400 sandbaggers wore life jackets stacking sandbags until the rushing waters forced them away. In St. Louis, massage therapists provided by the Gateway Massage Alliance rubbed backs, necks, shoulders and aching muscles of sandbaggers.

Whether they won or lost their individual struggles, these stalwarts labored without complaint. With the help of 1,000 sandbaggers who filled 250,000 sacks under the battle cry 'Save the levee," a 2.7-mile long earth wall defended Canton, Missouri, from the raging river. 'The feeling of pride and people working together – I don't expect to see anything like that again," said Kenneth Keller, who spent two weeks filling sandbags.

The Missouri town of Hannibal, population 18,000 and the birthplace of Mark Twain, remained largely high and dry behind a floodwall completed just two years ago. But the tourist town was also lonely. The bridges were out leading from Iowa and Illinois. Hannibal held its Tom Sawyer Days over the Fourth of July, offering such attractions as a fence-painting competition and a frog-jumping contest. But by mid-July, officials had to close the Mark Twain Cave, where Twain placed Tom and Becky Thatcher for a frightening confrontation with Injun Joe, because water closed an access road. The tourist trade was washed out this soggy summer from the Mark Twain Dinette to the Becky Thatcher Bookshop. Most customers at the Hotel Clemens during the peak of the season were from the news media and the Salvation Army.

The Mississippi swallowed Kaskaskia Island, an Illinois community of 125 inhabitants located 50 miles south of St. Louis. Kaskaskia was encircled by a 52-foot high, 15-mile levee built five years ago. But it didn't stand a chance in the middle of the river. To warn the diehards to flee, Kaskaskia tolled its 650-pound Liberty Bell of the West, which was cast in 1741 and is 11 years older than the Liberty Bell in

DELIVERY BY BOAT

LEXINGTON, Mo.(AP) – Here's the situation: You're in labor, but floodwaters have turned the minutes-long trip to the hospital into a two-hour ordeal.

What do you do? You take a boat.

When Cindy Taber's contractions began, she went to her local hospital in Richmond, but her doctor wanted her at Lafayette Regional Health Center in Lexington.

That normally would be a brief trip, but Taber lives north of the swollen Missouri River and her doctor and the hospital were south. Only one bridge was open in the river's 200-mile stretch from Kansas City to St. Louis, meaning driving would take about two hours.

Attendants were getting ready to load Taber into an ambulance when a paramedic suggested a boat.

"I said, 'We'll take the boat,'" Taber recalled. "My husband was very shocked. When the water first came up, I had said, 'We're not going by boat.'"

Minutes later, Taber, her husband, two children, two paramedics, the boat's owner and a helmsman were skimming over the water.

"The kids had a great time," she said. "They were upset they didn't have their fishing tackle."

An ambulance met the boat and whisked Taber to the hospital, where Brandon Eugene Taber debuted a few hours later at 7 pounds, 15 ounces.

The situation repeated itself when Heather Thompson's baby decided it was time to arrive. Thompson lives in Orrick, another flooded town north of the river, and her doctor, Manit Vajaranant, also practices here.

She also chose boat over ambulance. "She thought she wouldn't make it if they drove around," Vajaranant said.

About two hours after she arrived, 8-pound, 3-ounce Dalton Holloway was born.

An oil and water-soaked cat seems to have nowhere else to go as it tries to escape the flood waters in Niota, Illinois. After a brief look around, the cat jumped into the water and climbed onto the roof of the building in the background.

Snowball the cat gets an early morning rescue ride in St. Louis, Missouri. The owner went to his flooded house to retrieve two birds and the cat after the River Des Peres swamped his neighborhood.

Philadelphia. Kaskaskia Island was first settled by the French in the late 17th century, became a British possession after the French and Indian War and was occupied by the Continental Army in the Revolutionary War. The first capital of Illinois, it was forged into its current shape by an earlier spasm of river violence. In 1881, the Mississippi suddenly switched course during a flood and gouged out a channel to the east, creating the island and wiping out the original town of Kaskaskia.

A sudden burst of Mississippi anger broke plenty of hearts in New Canton, Illinois, across the river from Hannibal. The Sny Levee, a 52-mile clay-and-sand barrier, blew apart at the bottom after weeks of being pressured by the great river. It flooded 44,000 acres of farmlands and chased 2,000 people from their homes. Three workers on the levee were stranded in the hardwood trees, plucked from harm's way by National Guard helicopters that lowered rescue lines. The acreage was originally a swamp, but Missouri businessman Charles Clark saw the potential for corn, not cattails, a year ago when he led the effort to build the Sny. Clark believed a levee was the best way to control the Mississippi and make the property productive. Construction lasted from 1872 to 1875, but the proper design was never fully realized because of financial problems and floods. In the 1960s, the federal government spent $15.5 million and residents added $3.4 million to bolster the levee. The levee was raised 4 feet to 32 feet with the help of bulldozers and shovels. But all the work went for naught. 'That water has laid up since April. No wonder it broke," said Orville Wallader, 75.

The magnitude of the damage was smaller but the heartbreak was just as severe that same day in McBride, a Missouri community of 30 residents. When a levee gave way, the town was lost. The flood claimed the community's tavern, Al's Place, which had donated its remaining stores of beer to crestfallen sandbaggers. 'It's so damn hard to watch your life float away," said the bar's owner, Lois Neager, wiping her tears away with a paper towel. Her family had operated the business since 1947.

The Mississippi and Missouri rivers, the nation's two longest waterways, staged a double-barreled attack on Missouri. When a levee broke in St. Charles

A cat is saved in West Des Moines, Iowa.

How to construct a sandbag emergency levee

Filling sandbags:

Fill sandbags **1/2** to **2/3** full and tie at the top so bag will lie flat when put in place. (Overfilled bags leave gaps in levee, allowing water to penetrate.)

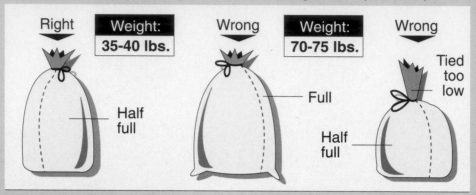

Right — **Weight: 35-40 lbs.** — Half full

Wrong — **Weight: 70-75 lbs.** — Full

Wrong — Tied too low — Half full

Placing sandbags:

Sandbags should be placed flat on the ground, overlapped, packed into place and stairstepped.

Elevation plan

Stairstepped   Overlapped

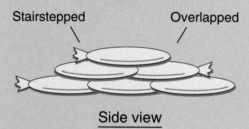

Side view

Top view

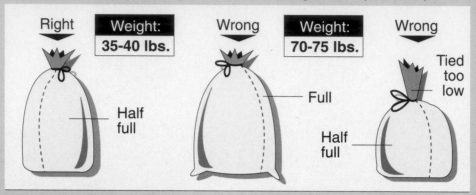

Polyethylene:

Polyethylene (poly) comes in rolls 20 feet wide and 100 feet long. It's used to wrap sandbag levees to prevent seepage. Poly should be placed on downstream portion of levee first, then worked upstream with a two- to three-foot overlap. Poly is held in place with sandbags.

Side view

Sandbags hold poly in place

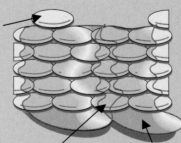

Poly overlapped

This sheet laid first

River flow →

Five feet is the practical limit of a sandbag levee. If a higher levee is needed, alternate means of construction should be considered.

AP/Bob Bianchini, Brian Sipple

A Jefferson County Health Department nurse gives a tetanus shot to a Festus, Missouri, resident in Crystal City, Missouri.

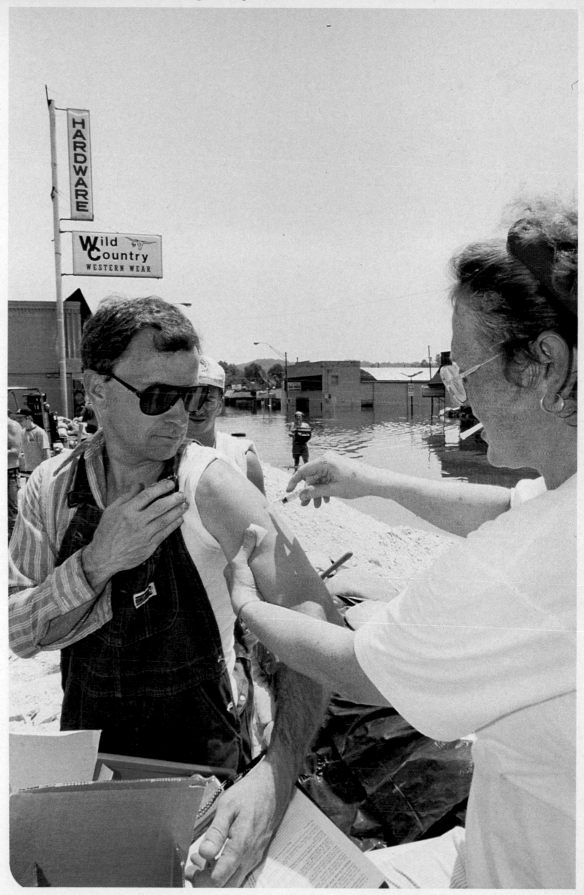

FAITH

HOLTS SUMMIT, Mo. (AP) – Though their homes may be submerged, their lives disrupted for who knows how long, the Rev. Myron Couch wanted his parishioners to know: God does not use floods to send messages.

"God doesn't prevent bad things from happening to people," the Baptist preacher told both his congregations, as they gathered together." But God is with us in everything we experience, and God is ministering to our spiritual needs now."

All over central Missouri, the Sunday morning airwaves carried similar messages of reassurance. Don't grieve, the voices said consolingly, this is an opportunity for you to renew your faith.

The message is one Couch believed the faithful from his congregation in nearby Cedar City especially needed to hear. He could not go to them; their beloved church is full of water and, like many of the homes swept flat by the flood, may prove beyond repair.

Lying on bottomland across the Missouri River from Jefferson City, Cedar City takes on water every six or seven years when the river overflows.

But the flood of '93 was without precedent, pouring over houses, mobile homes, businesses and churches. The town's 400 residents fled and remained scattered until the river slowly receded.

The Rev. JonnaLee O'Dell has sought to deliver the same reassurances to the congregations of the four United Methodist churches she serves, including one in Cedar City, which has water "to the ceiling," she said.

For those worshippers, the loss of the church – formed more than 100 years ago – has compounded the tragedy, for the church is a center of community life.

"What I have been trying to help people understand is that in the midst of this, God grieves with us, and that our faith provides us with what we need to come out on the other side," O'Dell said.

Couch's flock here is working to build a church, so both his congregations gathered in a local Lion's Club building. The two dozen people heard Couch read from John 7:25 about "streams of living water" – which the minister said was planned long before the floods – and sang hymns, accompanied by a portable electronic keyboard.

The men were in their suits, the women in dresses – even the worshippers from Cedar City. They knew the river, they knew what it could do, and so they had plenty of time to clear out their houses before the first devastating crest swamped their town.

After weeks of endless rain and ominous, crashing thunderstorms overnight, the sun shone intensely on that Sunday. It was hot. It felt good.

For Beverly Coots of Cedar City, there was no question about coming to church.

"It lifts your spirits to know the Lord is with you," she said. "It shows you that material things can be taken away from you and it's not that bad, because the Lord will provide."

A volunteer sits by relief food during a Sunday School service at the Salvation Army in Hannibal, Missouri. Some workers took a few hours off from battling the Mississippi River to attend services.

A woman and her daughter are interviewed at the Red Cross Shelter in St. Charles, Missouri. The mother and her three children were forced out of their home by Missouri River flood waters.

County, the Missouri swamped a peninsula and joined the Mississippi 20 miles upstream from its usual confluence. In all, the Missouri broke through in 100 levees and closed or battered 50 water treatment plants. St. Joseph, the stepping-off point for the Pony Express and the place when the outlaw Jesse James was cornered and killed, saw its 77,000 residents lose their water supply. Kansas City survived a thunderous collision of the Kansas and Missouri Rivers on July 27; both waterways had exceeded historic levels at the time. But the Big Muddy struck its most damaging blow on July 31, swamping 500 businesses and the Spirit of St. Louis Airport in St. Charles County. It was the most significant commercial district flooded in the state. Missouri Governor Mel Carnahan called it 'one catastrophe added on top of another." Ironically, the flooding and three tornadoes washed out a John Mellencamp concert scheduled to help flood victims. The Show-Me State was now called the Row-Me State.

St. Louis, the largest Midwestern city threatened by the flood, received a scare but stayed largely protected by a floodwall. Forecasters had watched the Mississippi crest twice at the Gateway Arch, which remained safe from its anchorage on a bluff, but more rains and raging tributaries brought a third crest on August 1. A 52-foot high, 11-mile barrier of concrete, steel and dirt – built after the previous record flood of 1973 – barely held back the river. But the current dislodged the floating Spirit of River complex, releasing a Burger King restaurant and the minesweeper USS Inaugural from their moorings. The complex smashed into the Poplar Street bridge and kept going downstream before towboats corralled it. Meanwhile, 51 propane tanks, each filled with 30,000 gallons of volatile gas, bobbed in the water at the Phillips Pipeline Co. The threat of an explosion forced an evacuation of 10,000 people, but a fireball was averted as divers secured the deadly tanks. 'It doesn't take long to get tired of this," said Diane Brayton Pope, who was staying at a shelter in a high school gymnasium. 'There's absolutely no privacy. There are 250 cots in there and they squeak. Every time someone rolls over it wakes you up."

Also on August 1, the Illinois community of Alton lost its battle to the Mississippi. The city of 35,000

65

Waiting for showers at the Altoona, Iowa, YWCA. The local water treatment plant was shut down by the flood.

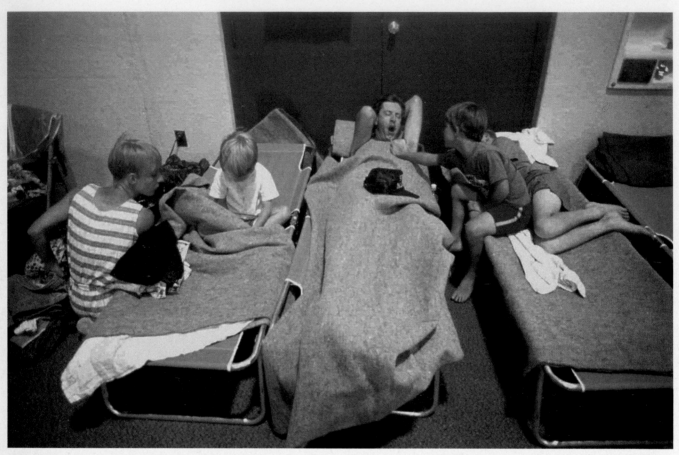

The day begins at the St. Charles, Missouri, Red Cross shelter.

ENTREPRENEURS

ST. CHARLES, Mo. (AP) – Ten-year-old Paul Tipton was scooping floodwater into a bucket to send to his grandma in Texas when a thought dawned: If this stuff were packaged right, would people buy it?

Within a few days, he had his answer. He quickly sold the first 100 of his "Flood of the Century" souvenirs – a 2-ounce bottle of Missouri River water glued on a marble base beneath a replica of the St. Louis Arch.

And thus did the great Midwestern flood of 1993, commemorated as well in miniature sandbags and T-shirts, spawn another entrepreneur.

"I just couldn't go to sleep the night I thought of it," Paul said, seated at the suburban dining room table where he and 5-year-old brother Patrick assemble the mementos.

Like many others selling flood memorabilia, Paul practiced capitalism with a conscience. Two-thirds of his profits on the $15 bottles went to the Red Cross and the Salvation Army.

Profit had become something of a dirty word in the flood souvenirs business. On the day he began peddling his bottles near the Arch, Paul said, "I was ragged out by a man who thought I was taking advantage of flood victims."

"That hurt my feelings," he said. "The first thing on my mind was to give some money to the people who need it."

Chas Anderton of St. Louis aimed to raise $5,000 for flood relief from sales of 3-by-5-inch canvas sandbags stamped "The Mighty Flood of 1993." He's donating two-thirds of his profits and encouraging hotel and airport gift shops to follow suit. The bags sell for $3.49 to $4.99.

In drier days, Anderton, 29, worked for a food delivery service, but the flooding forced a cutback in his work schedule. He had the idea for the little sandbags as he was helping fill the full-size versions.

"It's just been incredible," Anderton said of the response from gift shop managers. Some purchasers think the sandbags "are in bad taste," he said. "But I ask them, 'What have you done for the flood?'"

"The first reaction is 'Gee, these are kind of cute,'" said Hilda Callahan, working at the gift shop in a St. Louis Holiday Inn. "Then they get sober about it and say, 'Maybe it's not so cute for the people who are living through it.' But when they see some of the profit is going to flood relief, some of them buy it."

Around the Midwestern flood zone, companies that printed designs on T-shirts and caps were flourishing, with many of the orders coming from groups of volunteers or companies involved in flood relief.

Some of the companies were producing their own designs, such as the popular "Iowa: A Place to Row" shirt made by T-Galaxy of Ames. T-Galaxy sold 3,000 to 4,000 flood-related shirts and donated some of the profits, marketing director Roger Ossian said.

In Manhattan, Kan., a company called It's Greek To Me donated all the profits on its three $10 flood T-shirts to the Red Cross.

All other work was on hold at the company, which supplies T-shirts to sororities and fraternities at 220 colleges, chief executive David Dreiling said.

The attraction of disaster souvenirs escapes some, but Carol Griffin, owner of the Mark-It Top Shop in Jefferson City, has a theory. Her store and another ranch in Columbia were selling three shirts, including one that reads: "Been there, did it, rode it, bagged it, swam it, cursed it."

That shirt and others, Griffin said, tell those who see it: "Yes, we were there when this happened."

A child grimaces in pain as his mother searches for head lice at the St. Charles, Missouri, Red Cross shelter at the First United Methodist Church. Staff volunteers at the shelter reported an outbreak of lice and ordered people to be checked.

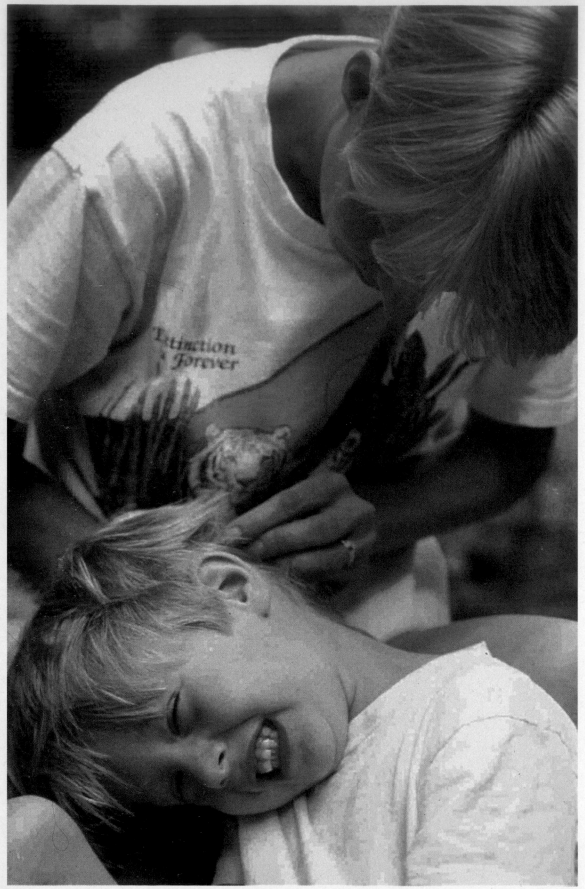

residents northeast of St. Louis waged a 25-day war against the river, throwing 6 million pounds of concrete, rock, sand and dirt into its levee with the help of volunteers from as far away as France and Hawaii. The levee held, but the raging river crept into the sewer system and backed up behind the sandbags. The mucky water inundated downtown businesses and knocked out the water treatment plant. 'Yeah, we lost. We won the battle head on, but the river outflanked us," said Mayor Robert Towse. 'Isn't it something? Water, water everywhere but not enough to drink," said Mary Eckhouse, a volunteer helping people lug home drinking water in jugs, bottles, coolers, buckets and plastic garbage cans. One of the flooded businesses was Tony's Restaurant, which has been in Paul Ventimiglia's family for three generations. 'We took a beating," Ventimiglia said, standing on the edge of a smelly lake that used to be a street. 'The water just does so much damage you can't imagine. I sat there and thought about crying. But we're planning on coming back."

Some of the most dramatic battles saved two historic towns on opposite sides of the Mississippi south of St. Louis. In Prairie du Rocher, Illinois, where French settlers built Fort de Chartres in 1722, the last 25 of the town's 600 residents had evacuated on August 3 as floodwaters bore down on two parallel levees. With little to lose, a risky strategy was proposed – tearing a hole in one levee to take pressure off the second, and then praying the remaining barrier would hold. The Corps of Engineers dredged open one spot. And when it appeared the water wasn't draining fast enough, local officials dynamited a larger opening. Two explosions echoed through the night, creating gaps of 50 feet and 30 feet. 'It was pretty desperate. We didn't have many options left," said levee district supervisor Richard Geubert. The gambit paid off, but it meant sacrificing tens of thousands of acres of prime farmland, a dozen or more houses and a restored French fort. Most of the farmers whose land was submerged agreed with the plan. But Carol Dufrenne yelled out when her 120-acre farm was devoured: 'We were the sacrificial lambs!" Volunteers in life preservers formed a human chain to pile sandbags on the levees. Among those answering a plea for help were a half-dozen striking coal miners who came straight from the picket line. One of the volunteers on the levee was Brent Pien, a Marine from nearby Red Bud. He was home on emergency leave from Parris Island, South Carolina, for the funeral of his grandfather and stayed on to join the sandbaggers. 'If we had something like this happen to us, I'd hope somebody would help me," Pien said. 'It just seemed like the right thing to do."

On the Missouri side of the river, the 4,100 residents of Ste. Genevieve waged their own valiant battle. Settled in 1735 during the reign of the Bourbon kings, Ste. Genevieve has the nation's best-preserved collection of period French Colonial architecture. It is the oldest permanent European settlement west of the Mississippi and connected in dry times by a ferry carrying tourists to and from Prairie du Rocher. When its neighbor dynamited holes in its levee, windows shattered and car alarms wailed in Ste. Genevieve. In five weeks time, residents built a sand, gravel and sandbag wall to protect their historic treasures. Their sweat paid off because the town, although soggy, was spared.

The emergency phase of the flooding faded into history on a sunny Sunday morning at Cape Girardeau. The river crested at 10 a.m. on August 8. About 130 homes were inundated, but most of the city's 34,475 residents were protected by a river wall that runs the length of downtown. A sign on the barrier read: 'We Love Our Floodwall."

The Mississippi River takes on a completely different character as it rolls past Cape Girardeau to Cairo, Illinois, where the Ohio River flows in. The lower portion is an alluvial valley, 20 to 80 miles wide in spots. The channel yawns deeper and wider, giving it a lot more capacity than the upper valley. 'The Mississippi is like coming down a two-lane in the middle of rush hour entering an eight-lane superhighway in the middle of night," Gary Dyhouse, hydrologist with the Corps of Engineers. Or put another way, it's just capable of absorbing more. 'It's like taking a bucket of water and pouring it in a wine glass as opposed to taking a bucket of water and pouring it into a bathtub," said the Corps' Robert Brown.

But the cleanup had just begun for a groggy region, which has been voted $5.8 billion in aid to help it recover. So much was wet, so much was

A flood victim gives a kiss to her 2-year-old son while feeding her infant daughter at the St. Charles, Missouri, Red Cross shelter. The mother and children were homeless after their home in St. Charles was flooded by the Missouri River.

More waiting and more rain for a temporarily homeless family at the St. Charles, Missouri, Red Cross shelter.

Residents of Portage Des Sioux, Missouri, attempt to read the mail and conduct normal business in front of the town market, despite high flood water from the Mississippi River. The flood forced most of the 400 residents to leave — only about 150 remained.

stained, so much reeked of river bottom and sewage that Midwestern dumps were filling up with the ruined remains of flood victims' lives. So much was thrown away that garbage trucks were gridlocked. 'It's kind of like the funeral after the flood. People are burying their lives," said Gail Andersen of the Des Moines Metropolitan Solid Waste Agency.

The future holds months, perhaps years, of scrubbing away the residue of a runaway river that has swept with it a witches' brew of raw sewage, drowned animals, fertilizers, pesticides, industrial wastes and all kinds of nasty filth. The muck gets inside walls and cars. It invades insulation, carpets, mattresses, sofas, chairs, stereos, televisions, videocassette recorders, dishwashers and clothes dryers. But you can't just let the affected items dry: everything that isn't trashed has to be washed, disinfected and deodorized to get rid of the germs and the stench. 'It's really a dirty job. There are going to be frogs and fish and snakes inside walls. It's going to smell. The problem with floods is the water just sits and sits and sits. The damage is progressive. It gets worse and worse and worse. This is going to be a monumental job," said Cliff Zlotnik of Restorx, a Pennsylvania company specializing in cleanups after disasters. His company helped clean Kuwait's Royal Palace after the Iraqis vandalized it, the World Trade Center in New York after terrorists bombed it and south Florida after Hurricane Andrew smashed it.

Some of the first places flooded have already learned what they face. 'Once the water was gone, we thought the flood was over. It's going to take us two or three years to recover," said Al Spaulding in Black River Falls, Wisconsin. Dorothy McKinzie, owner of an auto repair shop in Davenport, Iowa, rolled up her sleeves and held her nose, cleansing river bottom from her business. 'It smells like fish, and there's only one way to get rid of the smell: bleach, Pine-Sol and lots of elbow grease," she said.

There was also emotional debris to clear away. Experts who study the psychological effects of disasters expect emotional as well as physical and financial pain from the flood. Flood victims suffer a different kind of stress because the disaster has dragged on so long, said Elizabeth Smith, a professor of psychiatry at Washington University in St. Louis. With other

75

disasters such as earthquakes or hurricanes, and even most floods, the event strikes and it's over. Many people were under stress for weeks at a time. There was an intense feeling of helplessness and vulnerability concerning the awesome forces of nature. 'It's hard to see everything you own just slowly rise up and float away from you," said Don Nelson of St. Charles, Missouri, who was laid off from his job as a graphic artist and lost his mobile home to the flood. In Des Moines, John M. Palmer, pastor of the First Assembly of God, said those seeking help came with 'a sense of utter hopelessness, frustration, anxiety, worry. One guy just sat there and said, `What am I going to do?' "

The residue from the Great Flood of '93 will be around for a long, long time.

The Mississippi River creeps up on a billboard advertising a Tom Sawyer tourist attraction in Hannibal, Missouri.

WILD CRITTERS

HANNIBAL, Mo. (AP) — Just like humans, wild animals and birds in the Midwest have been chased from their homes and deprived of food sources by runaway rivers.

That means disruption or even death for ducks, herons, egrets, songbirds, quail, pheasants, field mice, rabbits, squirrels, deer, frogs and fresh-water mussels and clams.

All of them had fewer places to live to begin with because humans have engineered the flood plain for their own use.

"It's pretty devastating," said Phil Covington, wildlife management biologist at the 6,636-acre Ted Shanks Wildlife Area along the Mississippi River south of Hannibal.

"In a functioning system, the flood would have been a natural phenomenon. "This is a natural disaster made worse by man," he said.

Conservationists estimate that 90 percent of the wetlands in Iowa, Illinois and Missouri have been lost behind dams and levees, encouraging construction of shopping malls, farms and housing development.

So to provide sanctuaries, wildlife preserves have been set aside. But places like the Ted Shanks Wildlife Area are themselves under sheets of water right now, depriving their inhabitants of food and shelter.

It's like losing a rest stop on an interstate. Ducks, geese and other migrating creatures won't have a reliable place to eat, rest and refuel on their journeys from the north to the south this fall.

"The birds are going to have to fend for themselves. It's just going to be more difficult to find food," Covington said.

His area provides food such as wild millet and acorns from bottom-land hardwoods. But the flood tore open a 100-foot wall in a levee protecting the area, flooding the interior marshes and ruining the crops.

The timing of the flood is also catastrophic. The region has endured wetter than normal weather since November and was flooded in the spring before the summer rains fell.

That prevented many species from nesting and nurturing their newborns, and the youngest critters are the most vulnerable.

"We're simply going to lose a year of reproductivity in the flood plain," said Jim Matson, a biologist at the Mark Twain National Wildlife Refuge, which stretches 250 miles along the Mississippi from the Illinois towns of Rock Island to Alton. Much of the refuge is under water.

The exact toll on wildlife has yet to be tabulated, but the affected area includes more than just the Mississippi. Its tributaries and feeder streams stretch out like the roots of a tree leading to the main trunk.

"We don't have an idea of the total damage yet. But that much water over that much time has had a significant impact," said Matt Kerschbaum, a wildlife manager for the U.S. Fish and Wildlife Service in an eight-state Midwest region.

"The loss to human property and human life from the flooding is just staggering," said Bob Stratton, project leader for the Mark Twain refuge. "But the loss to wildlife and wildlife habitat is probably even more staggering, but harder to quantify."

One bird, the piping plover, nests on river sandbars. But there are no sandbars this year. They're all under water.

North of St. Louis, some whitetail deer were stranded on a levee on the Missouri. When the levee burst, several deer were swept away.

Like humans, wildlife becomes stressed if it's uprooted. But there are no Red Cross shelters for animals and birds. They have to seek territory already occupied by other wildlife - which is like being forced out of suburban Greenwich, Conn., and made to survive in New York City.

On the flip side, flooding can open up new habitat for wildlife and re-energize the entire system. It's nature's way of allowing things to thrive and recover, even after disasters.

If corn fields become lakes, waterfowl have new

feeding grounds. And if fish leave the river for new territory, herons and egrets have more places to look for food.

"Right now, there's a smorgasbord of landlocked fish for heron and mink," said Georgia Bryan of Iowa State University.

"It's kind of a give and take," said Terry Root, a wildlife biologist at the DeSoto National Wildlife Refuge, a 7,823-acre preserve along the Missouri River bordering Nebraska and Iowa. "If one species suffers, another one usually benefits."

A veterinarian rides a horse to shore after the horse fell off a boat while being rescued from floodwaters near Portage Des Sioux, Missouri. The vet jumped out of the boat and onto the horse's back to guide the animal in.

If you can't beat 'em, join 'em seems to be the attitude of these Missouri boys as they swim in the family pool while floodwaters approach from a break in the Valle Spring Levee in Ste. Genevieve.

A man leaps from the water to block a shot in Grafton, Illinois. The two usually play every evening but the flooding Illinois River has changed the rules somewhat.

Flood levels
Thursday, 9:40 a.m. local time

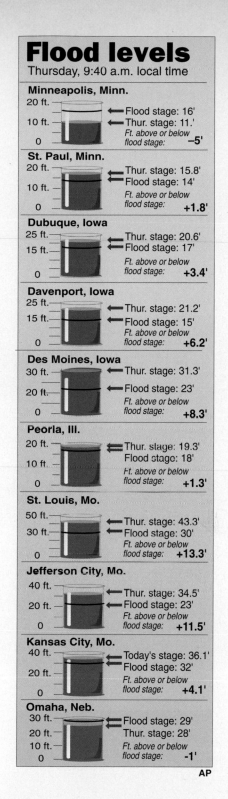

Minneapolis, Minn.
- Flood stage: 16'
- Thur. stage: 11.'
- Ft. above or below flood stage: **−5'**

St. Paul, Minn.
- Thur. stage: 15.8'
- Flood stage: 14'
- Ft. above or below flood stage: **+1.8'**

Dubuque, Iowa
- Thur. stage: 20.6'
- Flood stage: 17'
- Ft. above or below flood stage: **+3.4'**

Davenport, Iowa
- Thur. stage: 21.2'
- Flood stage: 15'
- Ft. above or below flood stage: **+6.2'**

Des Moines, Iowa
- Thur. stage: 31.3'
- Flood stage: 23'
- Ft. above or below flood stage: **+8.3'**

Peoria, Ill.
- Thur. stage: 19.3'
- Flood stage: 18'
- Ft. above or below flood stage: **+1.3'**

St. Louis, Mo.
- Thur. stage: 43.3'
- Flood stage: 30'
- Ft. above or below flood stage: **+13.3'**

Jefferson City, Mo.
- Thur. stage: 34.5'
- Flood stage: 23'
- Ft. above or below flood stage: **+11.5'**

Kansas City, Mo.
- Today's stage: 36.1'
- Flood stage: 32'
- Ft. above or below flood stage: **+4.1'**

Omaha, Neb.
- Flood stage: 29'
- Thur. stage: 28'
- Ft. above or below flood stage: **−1'**

AP

Flood data as of July 15, 1993

Record flooding
The 10 worst floods on the Mississippi River, as measured by water depth at St. Louis.

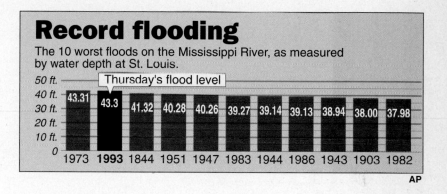

Thursday's flood level

Year	Level
1973	43.31
1993	43.3
1844	41.32
1951	40.28
1947	40.26
1983	39.27
1944	39.14
1986	39.13
1943	38.94
1903	38.00
1982	37.98

AP

State-by-state flood glance *(as of Wednesday)*

State	Deaths	Property damage	Crop damage	Evacuations	Homes damaged	Acreage flooded	Counties declared disaster areas (state or federal)
Illinois	3	Billions of dollars	$410 million	10,200	6,000	+125,000 acres	38
Iowa	0	+ $1 billion	$750 million	6,000	n/a	2 million acres	99
Kentucky	0	n/a	$4.9 million	Two homes	None	24,550 acres	None
Minnesota	3	$8 million (public property)	up to $750 million	n/a	10,000	2.6 million acres	25
Missouri	13	$500 million to $1 billion	Tens of millions	15,000	n/a	500 sq. mi.	49
Nebraska	1	+ $50 million	+ $117 million	n/a	n/a	+196,000 acres	3
S. Dakota	1	$8.1 billion (public property)	$572.4 million	n/a	960	+3 million acres	17
Wisconsin	1	$131 million	$125 million	500 to 700	1,590	n/a	37

AP

A Portage Des Sioux, Missouri, resident looks for drinks inside the flooded Portage Market. The store owner allowed town residents to pick out needed items free of charge.

THE ALMANACS SAY....

The Farmers' Almanac predicted the heavy rainstorms that battered the Midwest, but its centuries-old rival, the Old Farmer's Almanac, missed out.

The Farmers' Almanac called for everything from unsettled, wet weather in the Mississippi Valley at the beginning of June, to showers, severe storms and heavy thunderstorms in the latter part of the month. It also called for heavy rain and violent storms in July.

"I'm not sure if every single storm we called for happened, but it sure looks like we called for an unusual amount of rain in the central part of the country," said Peter Geiger, associate editor of the almanac published in Lewiston, Maine.

The almanac did not call for floods — which some say are the result of man-made levees, not natural causes. But because the almanac predicted "an unusual amount of precipitation," Geiger figures it hit pretty close.

A rival publication, the two-century-old Old Farmer's Almanac of Dublin, N.H., admits it was rained out.

It predicted "heavy precipitation in the central and upper Great Plains and in the South will cause flooding" this year, but that was for April through June.

"As I look at it, the mention of flooding in the Midwest in spring is about as close we get to it," said Old Farmer's Almanac Executive Editor Tim Clark.

Its summer forecast for the inundated Midwest called for about average rainfall in the northern Great Plains and a little below average in the central Plains, and there was no mention of floods.

"Nobody can predict something that happens once in a thousand years," Clark said. "That's clairvoyance, not prediction."

The almanac, which claims 80 percent accuracy, did predict Hurricane Andrew, was on target with the current Northeast drought, and did pretty well in forecasting what would happen in some East Coast areas hit by last March's Storm of the Century.

Part of the theory behind predicting, Clark said, is being "hesitant and nervous about what you might call 'remarkable events.' " Clark said. "That's clairvoyance, not prediction."

"The whole point of the system is to look at what normally happens," he said. The Midwest weather "is not normal."

The Maine almanac has 48 pages and is 23 years younger than the Old Farmer's Almanac. It is given to businesses for advertising purposes.

The Old Farmer's Almanac, first published in 1792, costs $2.95. It is the legal document for Atlantic and Pacific tides and sunrises and sunsets in most states.

A man looks over his car stuck in flood water near Portage Des Sioux, Missouri.

A curious sight in Lemay, Missouri.

A Des Moines, Iowa, homeowner searches his flooded basement for belongings.

CARP SHOOTING

WEST FARGO, N.D. (AP) – It's illegal to fire a gun at carp in North Dakota.

No kidding.

Outlaw carp shooters aren't usually considered public enemy No. 1 – or even in the Top 10 – but an unusual side effect of the floods ravaging the Midwest was a rise in carpicide.

Schools of carp were spilling out of swollen rivers and swimming through flooded areas of West Fargo and nearby Harwood, providing too much of a temptation for some fish-hungry gun owners.

All would be fine, except that bullets intended for unsuspecting stray carp could end up somewhere else. Like cars.

Lt. Arland Rasmussen of the Cass County Sheriff's Department said a stray bullet apparently aimed at a fish grazed an empty car. No one was hurt, but that didn't make it acceptable in the eyes of the law.

If someone really wants to make some carp's day, Rasmussen said, do it the legal way – with a bow and arrow.

The clean-up begins in Hull, Illinois. This home's furnishings were completely
ruined by the floodwaters from the overflowing Mississippi River.

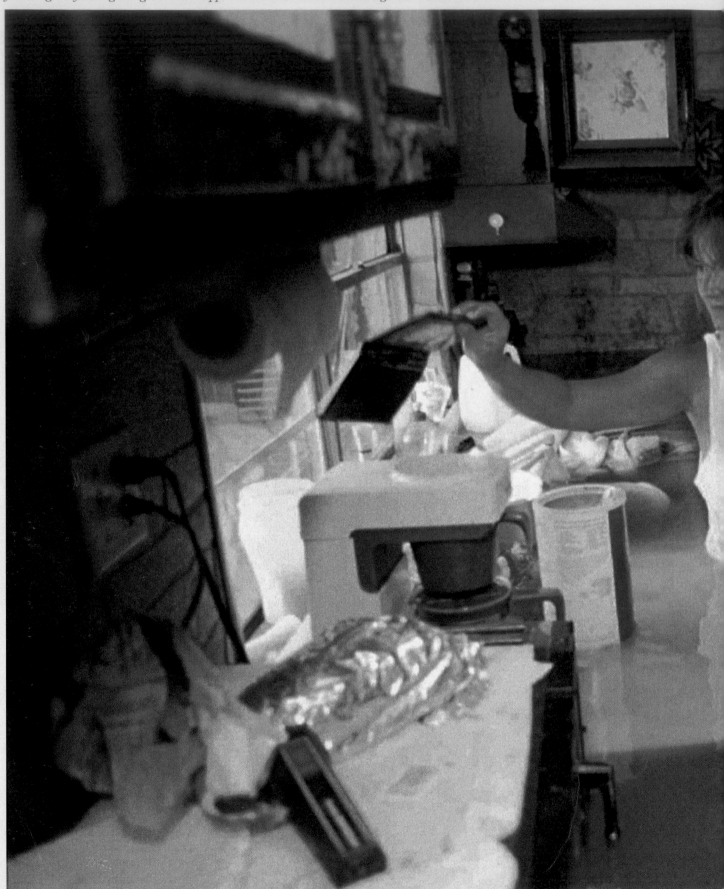

A portrait of despair in a flooded garage in Portage Des Sioux, Missouri.

LOST TOYS

DES MOINES, Iowa (AP) – It's hard to replace a 4-year-old's favorite toy that was lost in the great flood, but Don Lohean gave it a try.

"My office mate and I sent off a little stuffed monkey and a card saying, 'hang in there,'" said Lohean, a law student clerking at a St. Louis firm for the summer.

He and dozens of others were touched by a photograph of 4-year-old Heidi Ackelson of Des Moines that was printed in newspapers around the country.

"My heart has gone out to the flood victims this whole past month," said Abbey Gross of Indianapolis. "But this picture of a little girl holding on to mommy, crying – that got to me."

Well-wishers around the country packed up stuffed animals and others toys for Heidi.

The first box to arrive at the Des Moines Post Office was simply addressed to Heidi in care of her mother, Tonika Shirts. Instead of an address, the box had a copy of the picture that was photographed and distributed by The Associated Press.

Ms. Shirts and her daughter were outside their house, talking to city officials about flood damage, when AP photographer E.J. Flynn happened on the scene.

"We were down there and we took her in the house and she seen her stuffed animals were all buried in the mud," Ms. Shirts said. Heidi had lost Flower, her pet stuffed skunk, and all of her other toys. The picture caught her hanging on to a muddy piece of rabbit fur she named Fru-fru, leaning against her mother and crying.

"I didn't think people would think about a little girl in the newspaper," said Ms. Shirts, who works in a laundry. "It's really neat."

Their home was completely covered by the Raccoon River, which also inundated the nearby Des Moines Water Works. She said flood insurance covered $17,300 of the $20,500 she owed on the house, plus $5,000 for possessions.

"I'm a lot better off that some people," she said. "But we didn't have time to save anything, pictures or anything. We had 15 minutes to leave."

Holding a damaged stuffed animal, 4-year-old Heidi Ackelson cries after hearing that all her stuffed toys are lost as she is comforted by her mother at their flood-damaged home in Des Moines, Iowa. The little girl's tears stirred offers of help from steelworkers to office workers across the country. "My heart has gone out to the flood victims this whole past month. But this picture of a little girl holding on to mommy, crying, that got to me." a man from Indianapolis said.

A resident of St. Charles, Missouri, bales out the area near his home.

Damaged corn crop south of Booneville, Iowa. The flooding Raccoon River can be seen at left.

Lightning strikes near downtown Des Moines, Iowa.

Workers clean the Hilton Coliseum at Iowa State University in Ames, Iowa. When the coliseum flooded it suffered extensive damage including the destruction of the basketball floor.

THE CREST

ST. LOUIS (AP) – The crest of a river is explained simply: When the water rises to its highest level, stops and then starts going down. But predicting a crest is not as easy as defining one.

Nothing better illustrates that than the flooding in St. Louis. Forecasters gave a variety of crest predictions for the Mississippi, with each expected level higher than the one before.

But even then, they weren't able to pinpoint the crest until one day after it happened.

That's how it is with floods, forecasters say. There are so many variables, so many unknowns. And all it takes is one big levee break to destroy even the most sophisticated, computer-assisted forecast.

Crest information is vital for farmers, factories, towns and just about anything or anybody else along a river. It helps people guess how much of the flooding they'll get.

The National Weather Service determines a crest by several different factors, including rainfall reported in a river basin, a wide area that includes all the small rivers and streams that dump into the main river.

During the floods, the weather service also had to figure in the many levee breaks and the amount of flooding, since they help determine how much water is in the main channel.

All this information is plugged into a computer model, including the depth of the river channels and other data about the topography of the basin.

It takes all of that to come up with the predicted level of the crest – and even then, it is only a prediction.

The St. Louis Gateway Arch.

The Gateway Arch, its legs seen at lower left and right, stands on the bank of the Mississippi River. Tourists and area residents came to the area to look at the flooded river. The arch, St. Louis, Missouri's trademark, was safe and dry behind the 17-meter-high flood wall.

Sandbaggers constructing a flood wall in downtown Alton, Illinois.

Floodwaters from the Mississippi River cover the river town of Elwood with a blanket of muddy water after a levee north of the community broke.

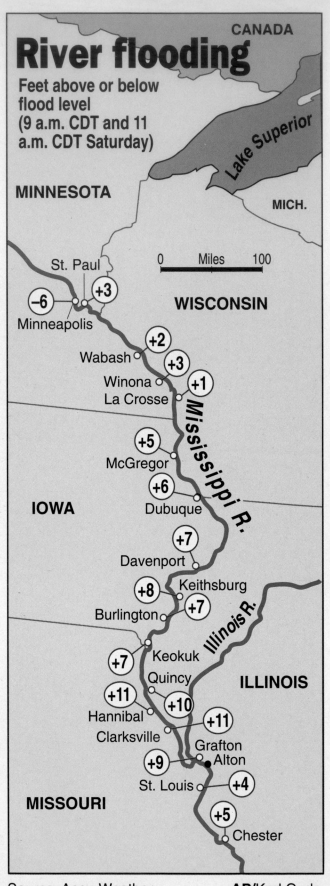

River flooding

Feet above or below flood level (9 a.m. CDT and 11 a.m. CDT Saturday)

Source: Accu-Weather

AP/Karl Gude

President Clinton hugs a young flood victim at a water distribution area in Des Moines, Iowa.

TEARS OF JOY, TEARS OF DESPAIR

ST. LOUIS (AP) – One by one, the three mothers who kept the vigil Saturday got the word from the cave. Which of their sons and daughters died. Which lived.

Nature's cruelty swallowed up four boys and two of their counselors in a torrent of water in a cave where they shouldn't have been.

And in the wake of the tragedy, what tugs at the hearts of the mothers of the youths and the counselors from the St. Joseph's Home for Boys is why the home allowed them to go to Cliff Cave Park.

The park had been closed for two weeks because of flooding from the adjacent Mississippi River. Barricades were up on the road leading to the mouth of the cave, a major attraction of the park, with the warning: "Road Closed."

On Friday, heavy rains caused flash flooding that sent water rushing into the cave's sinkholes.

The waters gathered force as they rolled in a fury through the cave. They overpowered the tormented, truant boys who had come from a home for troubled and abused children, who were down on their luck even before they became the latest victims of the great Midwest floods of '93.

Rescuers recovered the bodies of three boys and a male counselor Friday and resumed a search for two missing boys and a woman counselor Saturday. The three families of the missing kept a vigil near the cave in a blazing sun, hoping for word that their sons and daughters were alive.

One boy was lucky. He lived, and the word that he had been found alive filtered to the top of the cave. But for nearly two wrenching hours, neither mother knew whether it was her son.

"Oh Jesus! Oh Father!" cried Claire Vincent, the grandmother of 12-year- old Terril Vincent, as she waited with her daughter, Stephanie Vincent, who nervously paced the sidewalk. "Prayers go up and blessings come down. I read the Bible half the night and fell asleep with it in bed."

"It's got to be Gary," said Iva Mahr, the grandmother of the other boy, 13-year-old Gary Mahr, nicknamed J.R. He was sent to St. Joseph's for constantly missing school.

"I know it's Gary because he's a survivor," said Mrs. Mahr. "He hung on in there somewhere. I'm hoping it's ours but I want theirs to be safe."

"Oh Lord, please let this be my son," said Gary's mother, Sharon McRoberts.

Chris Ingram, an uncle of Gary's who helped in the search, rushed down the road to where the boy's mother and grandmother were waiting near a helicopter standing by to take the survivor to the hospital. He brought them the first word.

"J.R.'s all right!"

"Oh, God!" exclaimed Mrs. McRoberts.

"Are you sure? Did you see him?"

"They asked him his name. He stood on a ledge for 15 hours."

"Oh, God! Can I go with him?"

"Lord bless him."

"I still don't believe it 'til I see him."

"What about the other little boy?" asked the grandmother, Iva Mahr.

"They're still looking for him."

"I hope they find him."

"Good Lord, let it be him," said the mother. "Oh, God, how do we know this is him. Is that him?"

"That's Gary," said the grandmother as medics took him off the ambulance to the helicopter. "Take a look."

"Oh thank you, Jesus."

Mrs. McRoberts raced to the hospital by car to be with her son, who was reported in satisfactory condition. Mrs. Mahr stayed back to console the other parents who waited.

Later the word came up to them. Each was driven to the cave in a police car.

Stephanie Vincent, mother of Terril, a truant, returned to the top of the hill where the families were waiting. She collapsed to the ground in hysterics.

"Oh, my God," she moaned over and over. "I want to go. I want to go. Oh, Lord. Oh, Lord. Why did they let him go down there?"

John Lally, the president of Catholic Charities, which operates the St. Joseph's Home for Boys, acknowledged that a barricade did warn that the road is closed to traffic but that the home's vans were not driven past that point.

"No sign was posted at the cave indicating that caving was restricted or off-limits," he said.

David and Susan Metherd were the last to receive the dreaded word.

"Come with me, Ma'am," a police officer asked Mrs. Metherd.

Just three days ago, her 21-year-old daughter, Jennifer, a college senior and counselor, came home covered with mud and told her mother that she had been to the cave that day. She admonished her daughter about the dangers. Had she known she was returning the next day, Mrs. Metherd said she would have tried to stop her.

An hour later, she returned to where her family was waiting, including her husband who was in a wheelchair because of multiple sclerosis.

"She's dead," she said simply.

She embraced her husband, then laid her weary head on the window of her car, staring at a color portrait of Jennifer, blonde and with an engaging smile, that she had brought with her in remembrance.

David and Susan Metherd comfort each other after hearing the news that their daughter, Jennifer, a councilor at St. Joseph's Home for Boys, in St. Louis, died in a cave accident along with five male victims.

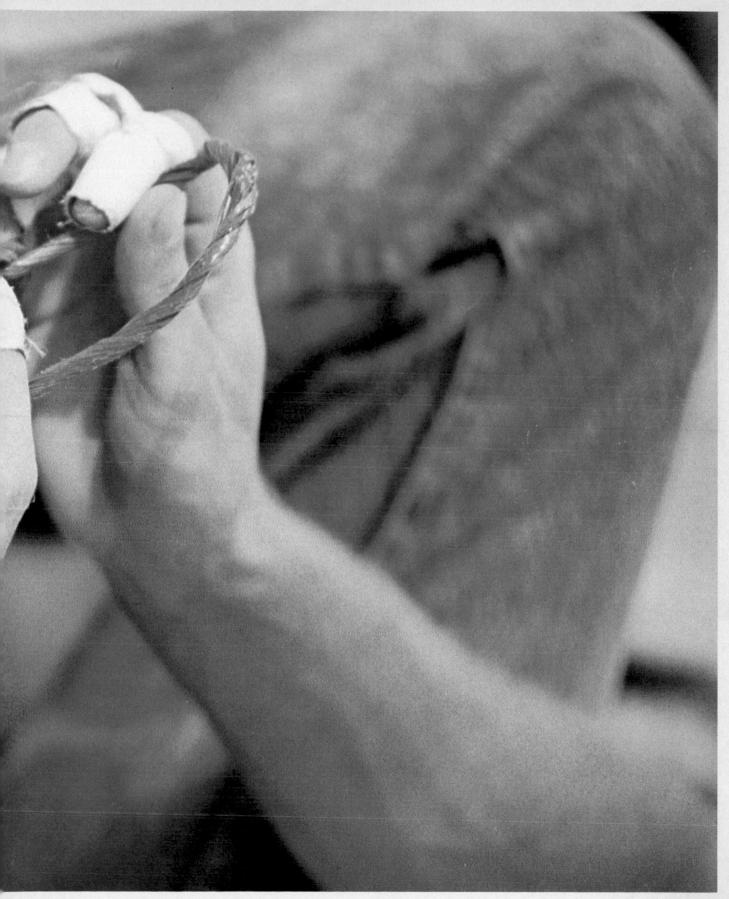

Great Flood of '93

MINNESOTA
Flood related deaths: 4
Property damage: approx. $51.3 million
Agricultural loss: $740-$990 million
Number of counties receiving
disaster assistance: 46

WISCONSIN
Flood related deaths: 2
Property damage: approx. $101 milli
Agricultural loss: $800 million
Number of counties receiving
disaster assistance: 45

NORTH DAKOTA
Flood related deaths: 2
Property damage: $100 million
Agricultural loss: $420 million
Number of counties receiving
disaster assistance: 37

SOUTH DAKOTA
Flood related deaths: 3
Property damage: $25.7 million
Agricultural loss: $725 million
Number of counties receiving
disaster assistance: 37

IOWA
Flood related deaths: 5
Property damage: approx. $1.25 billion
Agricultural loss: $450 million
Number of counties receiving
disaster assistance: 99 (all counties)

NEBRASKA
Flood related deaths: 2
Property damage: $50 million
Agricultural loss: $292 million
Number of counties receiving
disaster assistance: 51

KANSAS
Flood related deaths: 1
Property damage: approx. $160 million
Agricultural loss: $434.4 million
Number of counties receiving
disaster assistance: 43

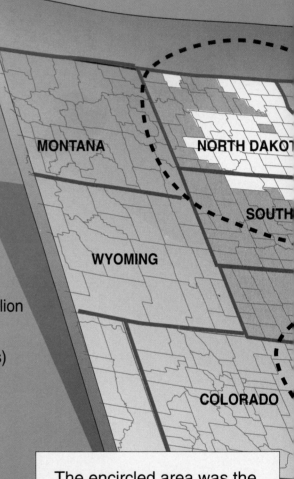

The encircled area was the hardest hit by the flood. Counties in white have received federal disaster aid.

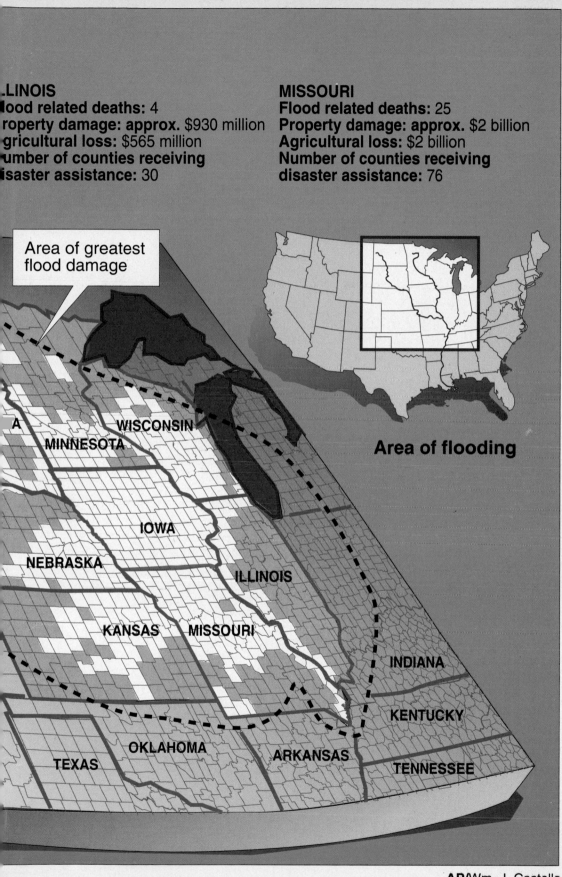

ILLINOIS
Flood related deaths: 4
Property damage: approx. $930 million
Agricultural loss: $565 million
Number of counties receiving disaster assistance: 30

MISSOURI
Flood related deaths: 25
Property damage: approx. $2 billion
Agricultural loss: $2 billion
Number of counties receiving disaster assistance: 76

Area of greatest flood damage

Area of flooding

WISCONSIN
MINNESOTA
IOWA
NEBRASKA
ILLINOIS
KANSAS   MISSOURI
INDIANA
KENTUCKY
OKLAHOMA   ARKANSAS
TEXAS   TENNESSEE

AP/Wm. J. Castello

THE FLOOD OF '93

In tribute . . .